ABSOLUTELY
SHOULD-LESS

SHOULDS

The Secret to Living the
Stress-Free Life You Deserve

Damon L. Jacobs

NEW YORK

LONDON • NASHVILLE • MELBOURNE • VANCOUVER

Absolutely Should-Less

The Secret to Living the Stress-Free Life You Deserve

Published in New York, New York, by Morgan James Publishing. Morgan James is a trademark of Morgan James, LLC. www.MorganJamesPublishing.com

Proudly distributed by Ingram Publisher Services.

Morgan James BOGO™

A **FREE** ebook edition is available for you or a friend with the purchase of this print book.

_____

CLEARLY SIGN YOUR NAME ABOVE

Instructions to claim your free ebook edition:
1. Visit MorganJamesBOGO.com
2. Sign your name CLEARLY in the space above
3. Complete the form and submit a photo of this entire page
4. You or your friend can download the ebook to your preferred device

ISBN 9781600374494 paperback
Library of Congress Control Number: 2008927556

Cover and Interior Design by:
Creative Ninja Designs
megan@creativeninjadesigns.com

Morgan James is a proud partner of Habitat for Humanity Peninsula and Greater Williamsburg. Partners in building since 2006.

Get involved today! Visit MorganJamesPublishing.com/giving-back

*Dedicated to all the clients
I have been privileged
to work with in
New York and California.*

T.O.C.
TABLE OF CONTENTS

- - - - - - - - - - - - - - - - - -

PREFACE
HOW THIS BOOK CAME TO BE

- -

W ho would have thought that something positive could come out of a financial crisis? Yet this book is the direct result of such an event. Back in the early 2000s, California faced massive cuts in funding to most social service programs, especially County Mental Health centers, where I was employed at the time. Many agencies found themselves with an overwhelming lack of staff unable to meet the high demands of the populations they served. I worked for one such county agency, whose clinical practices appeared to me to follow the guideline that medicating the poor was the most effective means to do treatment—with very little therapy and few psycho-educational tools being offered.

I vocally criticized this practice for quite some time. Once the money started running out, and hiring freezes were put into place, it became clear to the Directors of these agencies that the old way of doing business was not the most effective, or the most financially viable. It became apparent that the government could actually spend less money if more accurate assessment tools were being used, and if more therapeutic treatment was being offered.

Out of this revelation I was given the opportunity to run my own brief group treatment program. My mission was to give extensive assessments to patients just getting out of the psychiatric hospital, and to individuals at risk for needing inpatient care. I was to weed out those that did not truly need medications, without putting anyone at mortal risk. Within these guidelines, I was pretty much given complete creative freedom as to how to run groups and what activities I wished to lead during the day.

I tried many techniques to promote education and healing. But the presentation I received the strongest feedback from was the one in which we discussed the harmful and devastating consequences of actively practicing *shoulds* in daily living. No matter what problem the client came in with, no matter what diagnosis s/he carried, all responded positively to the concept of identifying the shoulds in their lives, and challenging their validity.

Some received such relief from this concept that they decided they did not require psychiatric medications. And those who did receive medications often reported a much easier time in life when they remembered how to live life "should-less." They reported increased medication compliance, decreased use of illicit drugs, less stress, and improved quality of relationships. If it could work for them, I thought, why not bring these ideas out of the clinic and into the bookstores?

And so began the wonderful and humbling task of writing the words you see before you.

My hope is that this book at the very least will remind you to *relax*. At the very best, it will help you to understand that every *should* that conflicts with reality gives you an opportunity to grow and flourish—if you search hard enough.

INTRODUCTION
THE STUBBORN SHOULDS

- -

Life doesn't have to be *that* hard. We are all in this together trying to make ends meet, to feel happy, to get along with others, to have meaningful relationships, and to experience a basic amount of safety in an ever-changing world. But for most of us, something is getting in the way; something is preventing us from living the life we deserve. We sense something is off, but we can't quite figure out what it is.

Despite great advancements in technology and communication, we have significantly increased our sense of alienation. We have so much knowledge available to us, yet we feel so much confusion. We have much more convenience, yet we feel there is so little time. We have so many opportunities to connect with others, yet we feel so alone.

This is because our thoughts and beliefs have become barriers to living life with the utmost fulfillment and happiness. These barriers are built on a foundation of stubborn *shoulds* that we are carrying at this moment. When these shoulds conflict with what is happening in the here and now, they effectively block us from being able to experience any of the joyful and stress-free living we deserve.

Shoulds are insidious. They are subtle, gradual, and usually not recognized until they have become severely problematic. All of us learned our shoulds so early in life that we usually do not remember how we learned them. But if you have ever experienced any stress or sadness from telling yourself you should lose weight, make more money, think smarter, look better, or be any different than who you are today, then you are suffering the consequences of oppressive shoulds.

The good news is, there is a joyful way to exist in the 21st century. Living *absolutely should-less* means taking responsibility for your self-destructive shoulds so that you may experience genuine happiness and peace. It is a thought process by which you train your mind to think critically, question ideas of what is "normal," and accept yourself and others without rigid standards and judgments. Being *absolutely should-less* is a commitment to enjoying a world without harmful shoulds, and a decision to inflict fewer shoulds on others.

By beginning the process of living *absolutely should-less*, as explained in this book, you will quickly notice changes. With a little willingness and discipline to challenge and alter your thinking, you will experience significantly clearer purpose, simpler everyday living, and more fulfilling relationships. When you begin to let go of some of your judgments and expectations, you will start to allow for more happiness, faith, and success in you life. This book will take you through each step, so you can effectively use the power of knowledge to question destructive thoughts, and take action toward having a much easier day.

Believe me, I know that making changes can be difficult. So many people try numerous things to feel better before they consider changing their thoughts: meditation, exercise, yoga, sex, relationships, music, watching TV, drinking too much, smoking, drugs, working long hours, getting more education, changing relationships, changing homes, changing diet, acupuncture, calling a psychic, or psychiatric medications. None of these is faulty or by any means a "bad" way to deal with suffering. But just by themselves, they are incomplete. I know, I've tried nearly every one of them!

I too have suffered the consequences of believing in destructive shoulds. In childhood, I was the recipient of severe and consistently harsh criticism by an angry and competitive older sibling. The messages I received told me that I should be smarter, stronger, more attractive, more articulate. The society around me told me I should like sports, should be more masculine, should get better grades. I invested in these shoulds; I believed they were true. But as much as I tried, I could not live up to the rigid standards of others. Eventually all these shoulds added together equaled one big thought: I *should* be dead. For a while, suicide seemed like the only escape from the world of shoulds I was living in. Fortunately, an intuitive part of me knew this suffering was temporary and that somehow, if I tried, I could find a more effective way to feel better.

Teenage years and early adulthood continued to be plagued with overwhelming stress, doubt, and ruminations which led to loss of sleep, loss of appetite, irritability, and fatigue. Sound familiar? Though I understood there was no should telling me to die, I still believed I wasn't performing the way I should, I wasn't living the way I should, I wasn't looking the way I should, I wasn't thinking the way I should, and therefore I was doomed to be miserable and depressed all my life.

Finally, in college I learned to question some of the harmful conditioning of these shoulds I had been carrying within me. I started to understand: the only thing hurting me was my own *belief* that I should be acting, thinking, looking, or talking differently from how I already was. The only real problem I suffered from was with my own perceptions and rigid standards of myself. When I let go of shoulds about myself, I was able to feel happy. I also learned that there was a political system and a financial industry that were firmly invested in me believing I was not good enough. Whenever I felt badly about myself, I was actually playing into the hands of these systems, and I had a choice not to. These concepts will be illustrated in more depth throughout this book.

I felt such liberation in learning these ideas. Given that I had a habit of "shoulding" myself about 100 times a day, I realized I had to do something to remind myself to stop thinking that way. For a week I walked around campus with a sign pinned to my shirt that had a big "SHOULDS" circled, with a line drawn through the center of it. Drastic perhaps, but I felt I needed something extreme to remind myself about the danger of shoulding. By taking such public action, I found that other people were interested in knowing what a "no should" sign was about, and were willing to question the consequences of their own negative shoulds as well.

Once I questioned and eliminated shoulds from my life, I also discovered that I was far more able to engage in healthier and deeper relationships with others. When I previously had placed shoulds on others' behaviors, I was limited as to how much friendship and affection I was capable of giving and receiving. I yearned to have longer lasting connections with others, but eventually my rigid judgments would get in the way. Once I ended the power shoulds had on my thinking, I was open to engage with others in a way that embraced compassion, respect, and honor. I no longer had to have a critical should about what they were doing, I simply needed to be responsible for my own shoulds about what they were doing.

CHAPTER 1
IDENTIFYING OUR
PERVASIVE SHOULDS

"But what's the big deal about the word *should*? It's just a common word people use to express themselves every day, isn't it?"

Yes, people do use the word every day. But that doesn't mean it is healthy or productive. There are seven major qualms I have with the concept of should:

1. *Should* assumes that there is an agreed-upon governing body of principles that we can all defer to in order to determine morality and standards. It assumes that you and I have knowingly and willingly entered into an arrangement stating, "We will both respect and follow the dictates of this system. We will agree upon how people should behave, how they should appear, what they should value." Outside of a convent or the military, is this true? Hardly. You are bound to encounter people different from yourself in this world, who have different values. All of us carry around our own governing systems based on ideas we have learned throughout our lives, and most people believe theirs are definitely "right." However, it is exactly this narrow faith in an invisible "objective committee" which leads us to condemn

5

ourselves and others, and causes problems in our relationships. In chapter 3, we explore numerous learning sources that instill in us the values we believe. Suffice to say, there is no objective moral standard for living that *all* individuals in a diverse world will completely agree upon, and so the term should holds no universal meaning. It's useless!

2. *Should* absolves the speaker of all personal responsibility. When you say, "I should go now," what are you really saying? That you have no desires or preferences of your own? By disavowing your own needs and wants, you never have to take ownership or authorization for your life. You can then defer your actions to that invisible committee that doesn't exist. This frequently results in blaming others for your problems and identifying yourself as a victim.

3. *Should* frequently encourages conformity and sameness. "You should act like others, dress like others, live like others, etc." It not only tries to squash out individuality and creativity, but it also harms those who are not able or willing to meet the standards that others appear to be living by. Children and adolescents deal with this in school every day from teachers and other students. Many adults continue to experience this in their work environments, families, even social groups.

4. *Should* positions your thoughts to be in direct conflict with reality. "I shouldn't be stuck in traffic right now;" "I should feel healthy today;" "You should have been home by now;" "It shouldn't have rained on the day of my party!" Notice how this feels. By telling yourself that something should be different from how it actually is, you are setting yourself up to experience unnecessary stress, anger, fatigue, and hopelessness. In

chapters 2 and 3 we will take a closer look at how your thoughts determine your feelings and moods. Suffice to say for now: if you are determined to argue with reality, you are going to lose, and quite often feel worse about a situation than you did before.

5. *Should* is an ineffective motivator for behavioral change. When it is being used to shame someone to work harder, make healthier choices, or produce more, it does not generate the intended results for any sustainable period of time. Many employers mistakenly operate under the belief that if they use "should" with their employees, then the employees will want to work harder and conform to standards. But do you remember a time when a boss has told you that you should do something? Did it really make you want to do it? In chapter 5, we will take a closer look at misguided attempts at using should to promote changes, even positive ones.

6. *Should* has always been used to maintain power imbalances and oppression. "The status quo" is a Latin term for "the ways things were before." Society has much invested in keeping things "the way they were before." Change is scary for anyone, especially for individuals in positions of power. Politicians, corporate leaders, religious figures—anyone who feels threatened by change—will tend to cling tightly to the status quo and use *should* as a way of manipulating others into doing the same. Every minority group that has struggled for equal rights has had to confront this.

7. *Shoulds* demand that we essentially play cop while monitoring our actions and the actions of others. They require us to spend great amounts of time and energy reviewing behaviors and determining how they should

be done differently. Historically, individuals in society were motivated to act in ways that would avoid incurring the wrath of a king or a god. Today, people are more motivated to act in ways that would avoid incurring the disapproval of their friends and family. Shoulds lead to extreme fears of embarrassment and social exclusion. We know that we will not get struck down by a god or legally exiled by a sovereign if we get fat. But the internal shame and social stigma can be far more powerful. It is this self-other regulation that causes us to walk around feeling anxious, alienated, afraid, and exhausted. Our bodies will not be put in prison for gaining weight, but our minds will.

Questioning, investigating, exploring, and challenging social norms are essential to living a happier life. I believe that when someone is going to therapy or seeking to be healed from their pain, it is not sufficient to look solely at that individual and her/his relationships, but to be aware of the world around that individual which creates, sustains, and profits from that pain. This is not a matter of playing the "blame game." It is just the opposite. When you have a more complete picture of how you have come to experience anxiety and depression, you are then able and equipped to take responsibility for it and take effective action to reduce it.

It is therefore important to understand how much of everyday anger, hopelessness, and anxiety originate from your own thoughts and perceptions of the world around you. What follows is a partial list of *shoulds* that many of us carry around. Check those you have experienced. At the bottom of each list, write in your own shoulds. If you so desire, please send me your contributions at www.shouldless.com. I'm always fascinated by new shoulds people come up with to torture themselves.

CONSIDER THIS:

Shoulds are like cigarettes for the soul. They may seem harmless initially—one or two every now and then may not kill you. But over time they become habitual, addictive, and toxic for your body and spirit.

I should:

- ☐ Make more money
- ☐ Be a better parent
- ☐ Be in a relationship
- ☐ Stay sober
- ☐ Read more books
- ☐ Have more sex
- ☐ Have more energy to do things
- ☐ Go to the gym
- ☐ Eat better
- ☐ Watch less TV
- ☐ Take better care of myself
- ☐ Sleep more
- ☐ Call my parents
- ☐ Spend more time with my _____ (kids, parents, pets)
- ☐ Be more patient
- ☐ Have more energy
- ☐ Lose weight
- ☐ Be more understanding
- ☐ Get more politically active
- ☐ Shave body parts

- ☐ Learn how to cook
- ☐ Drive a better car
- ☐ Look younger
- ☐ Wear better clothes
- ☐ Have more erections
- ☐ Be more on time for things
- ☐ Clean the house
- ☐ Pay the bills
- ☐ Please everyone all the time
- ☐ Get cosmetic surgery
- ☐ Always be nice to others
- ☐ Get a job
- ☐ Be more interesting at parties
- ☐ Volunteer my time
- ☐ Have whiter teeth
- ☐ Know more about wines and foods

(Insert your own here) _____

_____

_____

_____

YOU should:

- ☐ Meet my needs
- ☐ Drive better
- ☐ Pay more attention to me
- ☐ Remember my birthday
- ☐ Lose weight
- ☐ Be interested when I'm talking
- ☐ Be the first to say "I love you"
- ☐ Not steal the covers at night
- ☐ Buy me things I want
- ☐ Cook for me
- ☐ Like the same movies I like
- ☐ Make more money
- ☐ Shave body parts
- ☐ Stay the same person you are now
- ☐ Be more responsible with money
- ☐ Tell me I'm attractive
- ☐ Hang the toilet paper the same way I do
- ☐ Clean the refrigerator that we share at work
- ☐ Be monogamous
- ☐ Communicate clearly all the time
- ☐ Be on time for dates and appointments
- ☐ Learn how to dance

- ☐ Go with me to social events even if you don't want to
- ☐ Like my friends
- ☐ Give me orgasms
- ☐ Know when I'm in a bad mood
- ☐ Complain less
- ☐ Always look good in public
- ☐ Like the same music I do
- ☐ Call me more often
- ☐ Call me less often
- ☐ Have the same religion as me
- ☐ Put the toilet seat down
- ☐ Give me flowers spontaneously
- ☐ Be there for me when I need you
- ☐ Eat healthier
- ☐ Take out the trash

(Insert your own here) _____
_____
_____
_____

THEY should:

- Drive better
- Give perfect service
- Have given a different movie the Academy Award
- Be quiet during a movie
- Listen to me when I talk
- Lose weight
- Tip 20% all the time
- Be able to have legal marriages
- Not be allowed to have legal marriages
- Be able to get legal abortions
- Not be allowed to get legal abortions
- Provide more frequent buses/subways
- Keep my neighborhood clean and quiet
- Have more people working so I don't have to wait in line
- Speak softly on their cell phones
- Quit smoking
- Take more showers
- Respect their parents
- Speak the same language I do
- Stop begging for money
- Answer the phone when I call
- Deliver the mail faster
- Fix the electricity immediately when it goes off
- Always be on time
- Speak respectfully to me
- Dress differently
- Speak English
- Quiet their dog at night
- Charge reasonable prices
- Keep my favorite TV show at the same time every week
- Uphold my constitutional rights
- Not follow me around the department store as if I'm going to steal something
- Turn off their car alarms
- Eliminate advertisements from movies
- Remember ketchup with my burger
- Always have my favorite products available at the store
- Not tell me what I should do

(Insert your own here) _____
_____
_____
_____

If you are like most, you probably checked quite a few, and thought of others not listed. This is because we live in a world where we are bombarded constantly, and not always consciously, with rigid shoulds. This, for me, is living in prison. It is quite possible that you also are living in a lockup of your own thoughts and do not even realize that all along you have had the key to your release. Now it is time to start using that key.

In order to get out of this jail cell, it is essential to start to challenge the shoulds that you checked off in the previous pages, or any others that are currently upsetting you. This does *not* mean you have to reject the should or *do* any action differently. It simply means you are willing to question the validity of the should that is holding you prisoner.

Chapter 2 will offer you some guidelines for challenging long held shoulds, and beginning your journey of happier living. We will also explore some of the hidden motivations for not living *absolutely should-less*, and help you recognize ways you are using your thinking to cause yourself suffering.

Keeping these ideas in mind, chapter 3 will demonstrate how you can ask yourself six questions and make one statement in order to change or alter any should that is troubling you at any time. Prepare all your rebuttals and arguments, because chapter 5 will then address all the "yes, buts..." I've heard over the years in response to the idea of living life *absolutely should-less*. If yours is not addressed here, then please write me with your own, so it can be included in future editions.

Chapter 7 will address the issue of fear, and offer tips for staying focused in a world which is constantly telling us to be afraid. In chapter 9 I demonstrate how I utilize absolutely should-less thinking as I am carrying out daily activities and dealing with stressful situations in my own life.

At certain points I have put interactive exercises in places that will challenge your mind to work a bit. Please don't skip over them. It is by doing these activities that your perception can begin to change. I often find journal writing can additionally help when you are considering making positive changes. It can help you pay closer attention to your thoughts and feelings, and help monitor your progress.

Are you ready to start feeling better? Then turn the page and read on!

CHAPTER 2
GETTING READY TO CHANGE

L iving *absolutely should-less* will offer you ways to enjoy much better experiences in this world. The following will lay the groundwork for utilizing the tools offered in later chapters. Here are five fundamental principles that will aid you in coping with any depression, anxiety, frustration, or even anger that interferes in your ability to fully enjoy your daily living.

PRINCIPLE #1: THOUGHTS AND PERCEPTION DETERMINE EXPERIENCE

This is a concept we will visit time and time again. Most of us are conditioned to believe that we get upset because of other people or things. Try filling in the blanks below with three responses:

_____makes me upset

_____hurt my feelings in the past

_____stresses me out!

Now look at your answers and consider this: *you* have been responsible for your reactions to all these situations. Not the circumstances themselves, mind you—these may or may not have been in your control. But the *feelings* and the *meanings* you assign to each event are completely in your control and are your responsibility to manage if you wish to feel better.

For instance, there was a time in my life when I would take rejection very personally. If I was interested in someone who wasn't interested in me, I would immediately think, "I must be really ugly, no one will ever want me. I am a physically undesirable creature. I don't have it easy in social situations like others seem to. I'll never fit in. I'll never be attractive. And since I am such a basically repulsive creature, I should just do everyone a favor and stay home and watch *Golden Girls* reruns every night." Thinking these thoughts on a consistent basis was very much the source of much of the depression and anxiety that I mentioned earlier.

Then one night a friend of mine passed on some unexpected advice. Elaine was a very beautiful and very sexually liberated friend I had in my early 20s. She would frequently seek out new relationships and would, more often than not, find exactly what she was looking for. One night we were at a party and I saw her try to talk to someone she found desirable. Later she came back, sans hot guy, sans phone number, rejected. I felt so upset for her.

"Oh my God," I said, "How are you doing?"

"Fine," she replied sincerely, "Why?"

"Because you wanted to meet that guy, you went after him, and he wasn't interested in you. How can you be okay with that?"

"It's no big deal, my darling. I just wasn't his cup of tea."

And that's all there was it to it. She wasn't his cup of tea. It wasn't personal, it didn't mean anything. She didn't interpret that to be a sign of being undesirable or unworthy or of the apocalypse itself—he just wasn't into her.

In that moment I really understood for the first time that I didn't have to give other people the power to upset me, or to hurt my feelings. If someone wasn't interested in me, it didn't mean anything other than I wasn't his cup of tea. This wasn't a big deal. This meant nothing at all. I often got turned down after that, but came to understand that I had a choice: to decide that that rejection meant I was the most disgusting piece of crap in the universe, or simply that I wasn't his preference. Either way, my thoughts about the situation would determine my feelings, NOT the experience itself. To illustrate:

This was just as true for dealing with a failed relationship as it was for not getting a job I really wanted. Every situation in our lives can remind us that it is our thoughts and perceptions about a situation that determines our emotional experience, NOT the situation itself. Now, you try to consider that there is a different way to see that person or thing that really hurt your feelings or angered you. You will soon learn different ways to cope with all these situations.

PRINCIPLE #2: RECOGNIZE WHAT IS OBJECTIVE VERSUS SUBJECTIVE

One of the keys to unlocking that prison of suffering will be to keep in mind what is objectively true in the moment, and what is subjective. In other words, what would most reasonable people agree to be reality in this moment versus what is opinion?

I have a friend named Carol who tends to be overprotective of her toddler daughter. At the slightest cough she launches into a tirade of troublesome thoughts: "She shouldn't ever get sick; I should do better at keeping the house clean; I'm a terrible mother; I can't do anything right; she's going to have asthma and respiratory problems because of something I did wrong."

Again, our feelings are a direct result of our thoughts and our perception. Consequently, Carol experienced profound anxiety and guilt every time her daughter even had a sniffle. Through our discussions she realized she had a choice in this matter. She learned she didn't have to get so upset every time her daughter seemed ill. She later told me, "I realized I could feel better and actually be more useful to my daughter if I focused on what was happening instead of on the stories I was telling myself. The reality was that my daughter would sneeze, and that was it. The story was that I was a terrible mother and my daughter would be sick forever. Once I learned to separate reality from imagination, I felt much better."

This principle holds true for pretty much any situation or relationship in our lives. From standing in lines, to workplace dramas, to health issues. Any time you are starting to get upset or anxious, try asking yourself, "What is absolutely true in this moment?"

I have suffered from chronic sinus pain for several years now. On and off, apparently independent of weather conditions, foods, or location, it just comes and goes. But when it does hit, as any sinus sufferer can attest, it is bad. I started to realize, however, that I was making it worse when I attached a should to it. I learned that I could emotionally feel better if I could separate the objective from the subjective, just like Carol above. For example:

OBJECTIVE TRUTH: I am experiencing sinus pain today.
SUBJECTIVE OPINION: This is terrible! I shouldn't ever have to cope with physical pain. It means I won't have any energy today; I won't do a good job at work; everyone is going to judge me for being tired; I'm not doing a good job of taking care of myself; life sucks.

Do you see anything problematic with this line of rationale? Sinus pain itself just exists. It has no inherent meaning unless I assign it a meaning. And when I do give it such power I feel depressed and anxious, in addition to already feeling physically uncomfortable. Here's another way I have found to help cope with this:

OBJECTIVE TRUTH: I am experiencing sinus pain today. This means nothing. This is no reflection on me as a person. This doesn't make me good or bad. It just is.

Now, consider how often in relationships you tend to react to subjective opinion instead of objective truth. Someone doesn't call when they say they're going to. Someone is late to a date. Someone forgets a birthday or an anniversary. Your partner leaves their underwear on the floor. These are all objective occurrences that many people flip into a subjective meaning, such as, "He's a flake; she doesn't love me anymore; he's cheating; she doesn't care about me and never really did." Are any of these ever objective truths? Of course! But to decide that these absolutely are objective truths based on very limited information can be one way ticket to misery and despair, and will prevent you from living the stress-free life you deserve.

When you are upset or worried, ask yourself, "What is absolutely and objectively true in this moment? [Not in one hour or five minutes, just *right now*]." Then ask, "What subjective truths am I possibly making up to make myself miserable?" By getting into the habit of doing this, you are preparing to take the journey of living your life *absolutely should-less*.

PRINCIPLE #3: CORE BELIEFS CAN HURT IF UNCHECKED

So far we've been focusing on how certain kinds of thoughts can cause us much unnecessary pain and suffering. Although this is important, it is also just as essential to question the core beliefs that are *underlying* these thoughts. In other words, changing harmful thoughts is only part of the treatment. For example, imagine you were coping with chronic back pain. You'd certainly want to treat it with a heating pad, some aspirin, perhaps a nice massage here and there. But if you ignore the cause of the back pain, it will simply continue to persist and get worse. If you don't change the habits or actions which caused the back pain, such as twisting during movement or lifting improperly, you will continue to experience pain no matter how much treatment you have. Similarly, if you ignore the core beliefs that are at the source of your destructive thoughts, they will continue to arise and cause you needless worry and suffering no matter how much therapy you receive.

Core beliefs are the foundation of how we perceive ourselves and others. They are often rigid, distorted, and unconscious. Like most thought patterns, they were created early in life, and most of us don't even remember learning them. They become the filter through which we perceive the world around us, and the motivations of the people around us.

For instance, earlier I mentioned my experience of being rejected by someone I was interested in and the resulting shoulds: "I should look more masculine. I should go to the gym more. I should dress better. I should know more about music." The core belief underlying these thoughts is, "I'm unlovable. I'm not good enough. I should be someone different."

For added fun, I'd go through another series of self-inflicted tortures whenever I was job searching. Early on in my career, I had a very hard time getting a job in the therapy field. After interviews, my mind would automatically find dozens of way to replay the event: "I should have given different answers. I should have spoken less about this, more about that. I shouldn't have tried to make a joke right there. I shouldn't have worn that tie." The core belief underlying this thought was, "I am inadequate, I should change."

Some other common negative core beliefs we carry about ourselves include:

I'm ugly	I'm a loser
I'm stupid	I'm not as good as others
I'm damaged	I'm a failure

Some problematic common core beliefs we often hold about others include:

Others (or the world) should meet my needs.

Others (or the world) should change to please me.

Others (or the world) are responsible for what I think and feel.

The biggest problem with core beliefs is that they often become determining factors in our future experience. If you truly believe you are fundamentally an unlovable pile of garbage, then you will be more likely to attract and be attracted to people who reinforce this. You will be more likely to build a relationship with someone who abuses you than with someone who respects and honors you, because the latter simply will be so incongruent with your inner experience. It will be too uncomfortable and feel too foreign. This is one of the reasons survivors of abuse may be more likely to stay in abusive relationships. *Not* because they in any way deserve it or made it happen, but because their core beliefs about themselves can make them less likely to take action to keep themselves out of a harmful situation.

With that said, please keep in mind that not all core beliefs are negative. A lot of us have core beliefs that are quite positive, and help us cope with hardships. These core beliefs may include:

I am a survivor	I am lovable
I am smart	I am capable
I am deserving of good things	I am successful

Imagine how much easier life will be once your core beliefs are shifted. Much like taking the emergency brakes off a moving car, you will move forward with much more ease and grace.

CONSIDER THIS:

Underneath every (yes, every) should about yourself lie certain fundamental beliefs:

Other people determine what I do.

Other people determine what I think.

Other people determine how I feel.

Other people determine my value.

I am not responsible for my experience because others are in control.

PRINCIPLE #4: SECONDARY GAIN CAN KEEP YOU STUCK

Many simply refuse to feel better during the course of their lives. You may know that person who simply won't budge; they are stubbornly determined to perceive themselves as the victim, the martyr, or the one who has always been wronged. Quite often, they want you to feel the same way; to argue why you should also feel victimized. Or, many will craftily try to make you feel like a victimizer, the "bad guy." The last thing these people want to do is experience the joy that comes from living life *absolutely should-less*.

"Secondary gain" refers to the conscious or unconscious rewards of choosing to stay miserable. The intentional motivations are easy to spot. People may choose to be miserable if there is a some sort of financial motive. There may also be a reward of affection and attention one gets used to receiving when angry or depressed. I have counseled plenty of individuals who receive extra coddling from others when they display tears, rage, or insist they have been wronged and treated unjustly. Similarly, many simply feel more comfortable and familiar when they feel bad than when they feel good. It's simply a habit, one there is little investment in changing.

If you've ever seen a "Debbie Downer" sketch on *Saturday Night Live*, you have no doubt laughed at an example of someone who is stubbornly determined to be miserable. They feature a young woman who is obsessed with seeing the negative side of any happy or joyful situation. She is clearly in perfect bliss every time she says something terribly depressing or anxiety-ridden to a group of people. These skits are hilarious because most of us can recognize someone we know who is intently focused solely on negative aspects of a situation, no matter what is happening around her or him.

However, having an attachment to being miserable is not always so easy to discern or to recognize. Survivors of childhood trauma and violence often have needed to cling to a rigid set of behaviors and beliefs in order to survive. When someone associates pain with survival, then changing pain can be seen as a threat to one's very own existence. There is an existential investment in remaining upset, an unconscious belief which says, "I suffer, therefore I am." You can see how altering thinking patterns will be met with resistance, perhaps even hostility.

It is not only survivors of severe trauma who invest in misery. Why would someone choose to suffer? Think of it like this—when you invest in your suffering, like investing your money in a financial account, you will reap the rewards in one form or another (only secondary gain is much more reliable than stocks and bonds!). Here are examples of some of those rewards:

*Reward One —
Suffering Always Gives You Something to Talk About.

At a loss for conversation with friends? Well, you can always complain about your boss, your roommate, your parents, or the weather. Try listening to conversations of other people in the coffee shop, the gym, the supermarket, or the subway. Most of what I hear is how bad things are and how they are only going to get worse.

Talking about problems has become a fundamental means of connecting with each other in our society. We are conditioned to pay attention to what is wrong instead of what is right. Rarely do we grow up learning how to openly express things we are happy about. In fact, many children are told specifically not to talk about such matters, as it may appear "boastful." Movies and television most often reflect images of people talking about problems. Can you imagine an episode of *The Sopranos* without an argument?

Living life happily is not always entertaining or profoundly dramatic. When I give up my investment in suffering, one might argue I'm less interesting at a party, and have less to say. I sure sleep better, though, and have a lot more fun.

*Reward Two —
Talking About Your Suffering Can Give You Energy.

Don't believe me? Try noticing what happens when someone yawns near you. What is the first thing you are likely to do? If you're like me and most humans, you suddenly want to yawn, even if you aren't tired! That is because we are social animals, and our moods and energy states affect each other. Now, try noticing what happens when you complain about what is wrong to others. More often than not, you will feel a surge of energy, especially if the person across from you is saying, "Yes, that's right!"

I observed this vividly once in a work environment. It was quite early in the morning, and I watched two coworkers talking about how tired they felt. One started listing a litany of shoulds about the clients at the clinic, our employers, the scheduling, and many others. "The clients should show up on time, the people running this place should be more sensitive, they should hire more people, they should pay us more to do all this work..." and boom, what do you know, there was a new energy in the room. Suddenly instead of heavy and exhausted, the spirit in the room took on an electricity as we were getting pumped by this volt of righteousness and anger. The more secondary gain we experienced, the stronger these shoulds became.

However, I have also come to understand that talking about positive things can give us a boost as well. In the same clinic where I noticed there was a lot of energy used to talk about suffering, I started to experiment with asking people what they liked about their jobs. I noticed that although this took more effort, people were able to get fairly enthusiastic about what they liked as well. The difference was that now we were feeling happier, and more motivated to help the clients that we were actually there to serve.

Our moods do impact each other. Notice ways in which you talk about things that are wrong during the day, and try to be aware of how this affects your own energy level, as well as the people around you. Also notice what it feels like to talk about things you are happy about, or people you are grateful for. Feel which one is preferable for you.

Reward Three —
Suffering Helps You Avoid Responsibility.

People who see themselves as victims of the world never have to take proactive measures to feel better. I have always said that staying sane in an insane world is a full time job. When you play victim, you don't have to work at anything, especially not being happy. You get to decide that other people and situations will determine your mood, and try to manipulate them to "make" you happy. Then, when you inevitably feel disappointed and betrayed, you get to blame others for "making" you miserable. The secondary gain invested here is that you never have to take responsibility for your own thoughts or your own moods. You simply get to sit back and passively allow the world to decide for you. You don't have to own up to your errors, or the fact that somewhere along the way you made the choice to be unhappy.

Adapting a victim identity protects you from being aware of your role in problematic relationships and situations with others. The only downside is that it also guarantees you a life of tears, ulcers, and possibly an addiction. When you are constantly vulnerable to the words and actions of others, it makes the world frightening and unpredictable. Over time, such fear can take a toll on your body and spirit. Many people in these instances begin using a chemical substance to reduce their fears and lower stress. Ultimately they find these are not effective ways to manage the vulnerability which caused such fears. So what does work? Taking responsibility for your thoughts and moods is the first big step toward taking your power back, and understanding you are *not* a helpless victim of this world.

Reward Four —
Suffering Can Bring Attention.

For many folks, suffering and complaining is actually the only way to get the attention of others. Again, we are social animals, we all crave connection to other humans. What is problematic is when suffering is the only way one knows to get that needed attention and recognition.

It has always been common in our culture to focus on problems. What is unique about the last 10-15 years is that it has become more common to do this in a public forum. Television has come to offer a sense of validation and community for those who chose to be miserable. Daytime talk shows and "reality" court shows are filled with people lending public witness to their misery, and thereby receiving attention and a perceived sense of validation. For these individuals there is a clear secondary gain for staying upset and dramatic. If they weren't upset, why would they be on camera?

The same dynamic often functions as well in the workplace, and in our families. Quite often, it is the person who is doing the most complaining who gets the most attention, and may seem to be rewarded for this. But ask yourself, is this person really happy? Would you want to switch places with them?

If you are more invested in getting attention through your suffering than you are in being happy, then letting go of shoulds might be extra challenging. You may need to eventually ask yourself what you prefer: to be the center of attention, or to be happy. If you're interested in the latter, keep reading!

CONSIDER THIS:

Underneath every should about other people lie certain fundamental beliefs:

I know what is right for others.

My perspective is the right one.

My way is better.

If others don't agree with me they are wrong.

PRINCIPLE #5:
FAITH IS THE ANTIDOTE TO STRESS

Tragic events happen every day in this world. Just read the paper or turn on the news; bad news is always out there. In your own life you may have had to cope with some serious losses or disappointments. Sometimes terrible things happen for reasons we do not have the power to understand.

For a moment, take a look at the person you love most. Would that person be in your life if everything had always gone the way you planned? Would you be living where you live now? Would you have the same job? Think about the millions of factors that contributed to having the relationships you have now. How did you meet your friends? What if you had gone to a different school? Been hired at a different job? What if you had sat in a different seat? Given that things often work out better than how you planned, why bother having shoulds at all?

Living in New York after 9/11 has allowed me to hear about numerous experiences of people who were not in the World Trade Center Towers that day for one reason or another. A sick child. A broken shoe lace. An alarm clock that didn't go off. A long line at Starbucks that morning. One person told me he was arrested that morning. These were all experienced at the time as, "this shouldn't be happening," and now are seen in retrospect as life saving inconveniences. How many inconveniences have saved your life without you knowing it?

Conversely, what if everything did go the way you wanted? What if you had been hired for every job you wanted, had every relationship you desired, or had gone to every school you had hoped for? Who would not be in your life now? What experiences would you have missed? Any person who has obtained "success" in these areas can tell you it's not always what it's cracked up to be. The adage "be careful what you ask for, you just might get it" sustains itself because it is such an accurate and wise statement. If you don't believe me, try asking the most recent celebrity going into rehab this week. Sometimes getting what you want is the worst thing for you.

The concept of "faith" is about believing in something you can't see, and is generally referred to in spiritual circles as believing in a higher power. But whether you realize it or not, you are practicing faith every time you get out of bed in the morning. This is because any time you make an assumption about any future outcome, you are using faith. When you go to that not-so-beloved job of yours, you are practicing faith that there will be a pay check at some point, and you will live long enough to receive it. When you decide to live another day, you are practicing faith that life will continue to be worth living tomorrow, and will hopefully improve.

When you focus on how terrible things are in the world and how tragic they are going to be, you are then indeed practicing faith at these times, too. This type of faith is the kind that results in anxiety, despair and stress. Either way, feeling bliss or stress, you are using the power of your thoughts and beliefs to create your mood without realizing you are doing it. You can use that power to say, "everything is going to be awful," and then feel upset. Or, you have the power of your faith to say, "life is going to be okay even if tragedy strikes," or "life is going to be really wonderful," or "I will survive even if that person leaves me," or "I will be all right even if I lose this job," and experience the calm that comes with that thought.

CHAPTER 3
WHO SAYS I SHOULD? AND HOW CAN I STOP LISTENING?

B y this point you have read about the destructive nature of *shoulds*, the physical, emotional, even spiritual consequences they can have on you, and realized that there must be an easier way of getting through this thing called life. But how? How do we live our lives without shoulds?

It takes work, but it is possible. By going through the next seven steps and the exercises that accompany them, you can effectively reduce your anxiety, hopelessness, and guilt. Anytime you are in distress from one of your shoulds, you can ask:

1. How do I know this should is true?
2. Is this should true for everyone everywhere 24/7?
3. Who is profiting or benefiting from me believing this should?
4. How do I feel when I think this should?
5. What would one day be like without this should?
6. Who would I be without this should? and...
7. Now replace the should.

1. HOW DO I KNOW THIS SHOULD IS TRUE?

None of us is born into this world with shoulds. No baby looks in the mirror and says, "I should lose some weight," or "I should have saved more money last year." As a matter of fact, anyone who has spent time with an infant knows it is just the opposite—a baby has an intuitive sense of knowing it is a perfect being capable of giving and receiving great love, regardless of what it looks like or how much money it has. But somehow along the way, that infant will be conditioned with certain ideas. How?

What follows is a partial list of the different sources from which we are conditioned to learn shoulds. These are the people and systems that have taught you what you "know," much of the time without your even realizing that you were learning it.

PARENTS/PRIMARY CARETAKERS: Our parents or primary caretakers are our first teachers in life. Whoever raised you, took care of you, fed you, and changed your diapers was the first person to start conditioning your thoughts. We receive these messages long before we even start to comprehend language, and usually don't remember learning this information.

So many therapies focus on blaming the parents for problems as adults. In my experience, this leads to more suffering and dysfunction in the long run. Questioning conditioning from parents is not about assigning blame, it's about raising awareness. When you blame a caretaker, you receive the secondary gain of playing the victim, as discussed in chapter 2. When you simply inquire about your thoughts and increase awareness as to how you learned shoulds, you are able to take responsibility for them. The more you become aware of how you know certain "truths," the better equipped you will be to decide if you wish to keep them or not.

SIBLINGS: If you lived with siblings growing up, you are well aware that they can have a significant influence on how you think and feel about yourself and others. Young children are especially impressionable—their brains are like sponges just waiting to absorb new ideas. What they learn from siblings will have a strong impact on how they live their adult lives. Even in adulthood, patterns from childhood can continue. The influence siblings have on one another can be just as strong in all parts of the life span. That is why it is especially important to be aware of what those influences are.

EXTENDED FAMILY/NEIGHBORS: Now think about those with whom you had contact growing up, but did not necessarily live with. This may include grandparents, cousins, aunts and uncles, or neighbors. They may have told you how you should act, how you should dress, how much money you should have, the kind of friends you should and should not have. The values we receive from our families and our communities can strongly influence the values we hold later in life. Again, using the shoulds you checked off earlier, try to think back on early messages you received from these sources.

PEERS IN CHILDHOOD: Once you started leaving the home and going to school, you were forced to interact with non-related people your own age. For some this is a very happy and rewarding time. For many others, this can be quite traumatic. This often is when many children first learn they should look and act differently, with the implicit message being, "You are not okay as yourself." Children can be less than gracious about how they communicate such judgments; they are frequently blunt and cruel. Typically, this also is when rigid gender roles are defined. If you are a girl who likes to play sports, or a boy who likes to play with dolls, you quickly are corrected by peers as to what the appropriate roles for boys and girls should be.

TEACHERS: Along the same lines as peers in childhood, adult teachers can also have a tremendous influence in creating and maintaining should standards. Many children spend more time with them than their own parents during the week. Whether you loved them or hated them, they had a profound influence on what you were taught and the way you learned information.

PEERS IN ADOLESCENCE: This is a time where peers and friends exert a considerable influence. Essentially the term "peer pressure" would be more accurately defined if it were called "peer should-ure." There are decisions to be made about the way you dress, the way you act, the things you do, the music you like, how you perform in school, if you do drugs, if you have sex, or even if you go to college. These are just some of shoulds weighing heavily on the typical teenager, and peers usually play a tremendous role in these complicated choices.

PEERS IN ADULTHOOD: Think about who your friends are now. Who do you spend your leisure time with, play sports with, go to the movies with? Who do you go to when you need advice or help with a situation? As adults, we don't always pay attention to how much our peers influence our values and beliefs. Yet we are greatly affected by the actions and values of the friends around us. If you wanted to put this to the test, try doing something different from what your friends expect of you. What if you didn't send out Christmas or holiday cards this year? What if you dyed your hair a different color? What if you took up a completely new hobby? How do you think your friends would respond? Some may be very supportive and encourage you to try new things and grow. But many others have peers who are not so supportive and embracing of change. Try recognizing the effects of your friendships in your own life, and the shoulds that may be affecting you without you even realizing it.

SPOUSES/PARTNERS: This may appear obvious from the outset, yet quite often when two people are in a relationship, they are not always aware of how strongly they are affecting each other. It is often the person closest to you who bears the brunt of your unquestioned shoulds. For example, if I was raised to believe that I should never communicate my feelings, then I will carry that into a relationship, and put that should on my partner as well. That partner may then feel judged and shamed for trying to communicate his feelings, and next time say to himself, "I shouldn't talk about such things." In this way, people in intimate relationships sometimes exert shoulds that leads to hurt, stress, and resentment.

COWORKERS: Most of us have to work with others, and have to find ways to get along. There are times when you may have to spend eight to nine hours a day with your coworkers, which is usually more waking time than you spend with your family. For this reason, coworkers often exert a considerable influence on you, without us even realizing it. They may influence the way you dress for work, answer the phone, where you spend your lunches, or what you do for fun after work. They may affect your attitude about the employers you work for, and how you deal with conflict and stress. If it's hard to recognize these shoulds right now, just wait until you do something which goes against them. I once was told I shouldn't be so friendly on the phone! Before that I had no awareness that it was the clinic's should to respond in a cool detached way. What are the shoulds affecting you in your work environment?

CULTURE/ETHNICITY: Depending on your cultural or ethnic background, you may also have been raised with some clear rules or guidelines about the way you should live your life as a child, and as an adult. Culture operates differently from relationships listed previously, as it involves groups of people influencing you instead of just the individuals in your life. You may have been given messages from your culture(s) as to who you should and shouldn't love, where you should and shouldn't live, what kinds of things you should and shouldn't do in your spare time, what kind of work you should or shouldn't do. Many of these ideas may oppose each other, resulting in significant stress and confusion.

For instance, Sylvia is raised in a working class Hispanic family in East Los Angeles. She learns from her family that she should get an education, obey authority, and fulfill her role as a woman by getting married and raising children. She goes to a college where she learns she should question authority, squander money, and reject the traditional notions of marriage and motherhood. How does she navigate these conflicting ideas?

Bradley is a raised in a traditional African American family in Harlem. He learns that being a man means he should bury his feelings inside, use drugs to cope with his emotions, use violence to handle conflicts, and that the most important thing is to make money. After an encounter with the law, he goes into a treatment program where he learns that being a man means he should openly express his feelings, not use drugs to cope with emotions, not use violence in arguments, and that staying alive and healthy is more important than making a lot of money.

These examples illustrate how all of us operate in and out of the different cultures throughout our lives. We have our family cultures, neighborhood cultures, ethnic cultures, work and school cultures, and many others. It can feel quite stressful when you are functioning in two or more cultures with oppositional values. The first step toward finding more peace is simply to be aware of how culture has affected your values in the past and present. Try asking yourself, "Do I hold cultural shoulds now that are harming me in any way? Am I willing to let go of them if it would help me feel better?"

MEDIA: This is perhaps the most pervasive and dangerous of all the sources we have listed so far. It is so insidious and so present, most of us don't realize how manipulated and controlled we are by media standards every day.

Any magazine you read, any newspaper you open, any TV show you turn on is bombarding your senses with overwhelming messages that "you are not good enough, you should look/act/feel different." According to mainstream media, you should be white, you should be thin, you should be rich, you should be young, you should be healthy, you should be heterosexual, you should be happy, you should be drug free, you should be productive, you should be interested in sex (but not too interested if you're a woman or a gay man), you should be articulate, you should have whiter teeth, cleaner kitchens, newer cars, wrinkle free clothes, wrinkle free skin, and if you don't then no one can ever possibly like or accept you.

Keep in mind, the entire multibillion-dollar advertising industry can operate only if you believe there is something deficient about who you are and that you should buy products in order to change something about yourself. If you did not feel like there was something fundamentally unlovable or inadequate about who you are, then there would be no need to purchase anything beyond the basic necessities.

GOVERNMENT: Like it or not, government plays a large role in how people form shoulds about themselves and about the community around them. Laws concerning marriage, drugs, and right-to-die issues are frequently debated in local, state, and federal arenas. Once laws are passed, they become "shoulds" of public consciousness.

For example, heroin was once an accepted staple of American life, and was sold openly as a pain reliever until it was banned by U.S. Congress in 1905. What followed directly from this was a judgmental should against individuals addicted to opiates, which continues today. Such condemnation only adds to the shame of addiction, which makes it much harder for someone to believe they are deserving of healthier choices.

Until the 1950s, most American states had anti-miscegenation laws, which forbade a man and a woman of two different races to marry. Many states continued to uphold such laws until 1967, giving the clear message that two people of different races should not love and live together. Today, most states uphold laws forbidding two people of the same gender to legally marry, thereby communicating the strong message, "gays and lesbians should not have equal rights and equal protections."

Whether or not you agree or disagree with these laws, the point is simply to note that government practices do have an effect on individual shoulds. History has consistently demonstrated that when laws change, attitudes change as well.

SOCIETAL NORMS: Interwoven with politics are societal standards and norms. Some directly impact lawmaking policies, as mentioned above. Others are less formalized, but no less insidious.

Gender roles, for instance, are heavily enforced in most schools. Boys should not cry and girls should not yell. Girls should not prefer sports to dolls and boys should not prefer dolls to sports. Boys should compete, girls should play co-operatively. As adults, we receive clear messages as well. It may not be illegal for a man to wear a dress, but in most areas it will certainly create a disturbance and could be downright deadly in others. In fact, a teenage boy was tragically murdered in Florida in February, 2008, allegedly for simply wearing a dress in public.

Many societal shoulds are concepts we don't even think about. You should stare forward in an elevator. You should answer the phone "Hello?" You should sit down at a restaurant before ordering. You should use certain utensils at certain times in meals. In New York, I have had it pointed out to me several times that I should stick to the right side when passing people on the sidewalk or going down stairs in the subway station.

The tricky part about societal shoulds is that they change. And they change frequently! Just a few years ago, many considered it desperate to use a computer dating service to meet someone. Now, many agree it is time-efficient, safe, effective, and preferable to the some of the more grueling forms of artificial socializing or bar hopping. It used to be a given that people would dress up if they were traveling; now most people choose to dress comfortably. It used to be a sign of insanity to walk down the street talking to yourself; now with handsfree cell phones it is commonplace. If today's judgment is accepted as normal tomorrow, why bother shoulding or condemning anything at all?

RELIGION: For many people, religion is a powerful and intense means of learning shoulds very early in life. From marriage to masturbation, from abortions to zygotes, religion provides a solid framework for many rigid, inflexible, and sometimes, harmful shoulds.

Now, before you throw this book across the room and demand that you "should" get your money back, let me be clear about something: Religion can be a source of tremendous comfort, stability, and happiness for many individuals. The 10 Commandments, the "thou shalt not's..." provide a needed sense of structure and meaning for millions of high functioning intelligent adults.

But for millions, religion is a source of confusion, conflict, and despair. It sets up a system of shoulds in which one's own desires and preferences are promptly and swiftly shamed and denied. It prevents an individual from being true to oneself, which frequently results in tension, anxiety, and even suicidal hopelessness. I'm not saying this always happens, but as a therapist I see it frequently.

Did you see in these last few pages the dozens (maybe hundreds) of messages you have received about how you should live your life, what you should do, what you should think, and how you should look? Notice if any of the messages you have received contradict each other. Keep in mind, this is only a partial list of sources that influence our thinking.

You may already have thought of others not listed. Although thinking about all these messages can be an overwhelming task, it serves the purpose of getting you to stand away from your conditioning just long enough to decide if a value is helpful for you, or hurtful. Does a message you have learned bring you joy or pain? Only you can truly decide this.

Now, imagine if someone you knew did the same exercises. What might their answers be? What if your partner did them, or your parents, or your boss? You would no doubt see some very different responses to the same questions. This is because we are all raised differently. None of us, not even a brother or sister, will have the same experiences and the same responses to them. We are all unique individuals who have acquired different shoulds in different ways. Given this truth, how is it possible that one should could truly exist? Since no two people have learned the exact same values, and therefore everyone's shoulds are going to be different, how is it possible for one person to say that their should is more valid?

It's like licking an ice cream cone—everyone has their own way of doing this that is personally right for them. So how could one way be the "right" way? The same holds true for how we look, how we think, how we eat, how we make love. There is no universal consensus that holds true for these issues. No matter where you go, someone is going to agree with you, and someone won't, so why spend so much time consumed with panic or worry that you're getting it wrong? And why go around trying to make others conform to a standard that is so different for each individual?

What follows is the first exercise in helping you identify and challenge any should that is causing you any pain or suffering. Once you begin to recognize sources of learning, you are ready to make a Should Pie. A Should Pie is simply a should with a circle around it surrounded by other circles containing the source of this should. For example:

EXERCISE: Think about the should that is troubling you the most today. Write it down below:

_____

_____

_____

Now use the space below to make your own Should Pie. I've included five circles for each should, but you may not need that many, or you may want to include more. It is up to you to do them as you see fit.

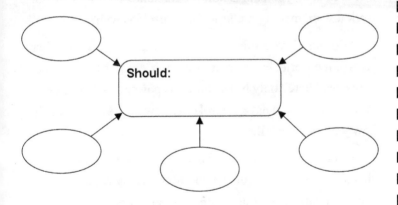

2. IS THIS SHOULD TRUE FOR EVERYONE, EVERYWHERE, 24/7?

Continue now with the should you wrote in the last exercise. Ask yourself: Is this should true for me? Is it true for your child? Your parent? Your neighbor? For women and men everywhere in the world? All the time? How can any of us definitely know such a thing?

The reason this question is important is because it encourages us to examine cultural context and diversity. Let's look again at the should, "I should lose some weight." Is this true for everyone everywhere? Are there happy people somewhere who don't believe this? Is thin considered to be the epitome of beauty and power everywhere in the world? If a should that is causing you pain is not true for someone else, why not work toward making it untrue for yourself as well?

"Because," you might say, "that might be true in other parts of the world, but we don't live there, we live here." True. However, "here" only has as much as power as you decide to give it. You do not have control over how others see you, only how you see yourself.

Choosing to speak out against a value as entrenched as "I should lose some weight" could unfortunately result in some social embarrassment and ostracization. It usually involves going completely against what society expects of you. Keep in mind, however, Gandhi, Martin Luther King, Jr., Rosa Parks, and Princess Diana of Wales. All had to go against the tide of the society in their times as well. They had to break social taboos and challenge the structure in order to live an authentic, peaceful, and meaningful life. By being true to themselves, they helped millions of others. You too are in the position of being a catalyst for positive change in your own environment, just by challenging assumed notions such as, "I should lose weight."

Now ask yourself the question again. If your should doesn't apply to everyone everywhere in the world, then why does it apply to you? It can't if you don't give it the power.

_____

_____

EXERCISE:

This exercise is intended to help you with the question, "Is this should true for everyone everywhere 24/7?" One of the essential ways of challenging your should is recognizing how it may not apply to everyone else on the planet at this moment. Look at the should you wrote down, and try asking yourself the following questions:

Does this should apply to everyone with the same gender as yourself? _____

Does this should apply to everyone the same age as you?

_____

Does this should apply to everyone who lives near you?

_____

Does this should apply to everyone living in every country in the world? _____

Does the same should apply to everyone of the opposite gender? _____

Have you ever known anyone who didn't have the same should as you who was happy? Who?

_____

_____

_____

_____

Is it possible for anyone to live without this should and still be happy? How?

_____

_____

_____

_____

_____

_____

Why is it that some rules may apply to some, but not others?

_____

_____

_____

_____

_____

_____

_____

3. WHO IS PROFITING OR BENEFITING FROM MY SHOULD?

Anytime you are suffering because of a should, there is someone benefiting somewhere. Who are these someones, and how are are they profiting? Go back to the Should Pie and look—you may begin to find some answers there.

The media is the most blatant example. The very purpose of advertising in any area is to communicate to you, "You are not okay as you are, you should be different." The idea "I should lose weight" is particularly susceptible to this, since this notion has been unquestionably drilled into the mind of nearly every young girl and many young boys before their brains could fully grasp what it even meant. Every time you believe ads and buy a product, you are supporting a billion dollar industry that is invested in *always* making you feel you are not good enough. According to a report on Cosmeticsbusiness.com, the Avon company alone earned *8.8 billion dollars* in 2006.[1] They could not gross that much if people challenged the shoulds they were receiving from advertising and entertainment.

I'm not saying there's anything "wrong" with purchasing cosmetic products or losing weight. What I am saying is that it is important, for the sake of your mental and emotional well being, to know *why* you are buying them or why you are losing pounds. I have a friend who decided to have cosmetic surgery to get rid of the bags under her eyes. For her this was truly an action based on love for herself. It's something she wanted, not needed, and it helped her—not "made" her—feel better. I have another friend who at age 42 discovered Botox. She did not want to get it, she did not like the feeling of it.

---

[1] Cosmetics Business.com: "Avon on Road to Recovery." (accessed April 25, 2007)

But she felt she should do it if she ever wanted to get married. Her action was out of a should based in fear of being single, i.e., "I should change myself so I'm not alone the rest of my life." She was constantly sad, hopeless, and anxious that if she didn't continue with these treatments, she would not find a partner. Ironically, it was this very fear and self-loathing that drove men away from her, even with a smooth forehead.

But profits from shoulds are not only monetary. As mentioned in chapter 1, society depends on a certain level of "status quo" in order to keep the peace. We all have a vested interest in keeping some rules the same, such as, "You should stop at a red light when driving." It is when these rules result in oppressive shoulds that they need to be challenged. This is exactly what the Women's, Civil Rights, and Gay/Lesbian movements did during the 1960s and 1970s. Can you think of any political groups today that are challenging the shoulds of the status quo? Who is profiting by trying to keep things the same?

Of course, profit is not always obvious, and certainly not always malicious. In our families and in our relationships there are quite often non-spoken shoulds which help preserve order. For example, members of families generally take on roles such as the "sick one," the "healthy one," the "joker," or the "distant" one. "Homeostasis" is a term used in couple/family therapy referring to the tendency we humans have to keep interpersonal patterns the same. The benefit is that by keeping the family status quo no one has to take responsibility for questioning their own actions or do anything differently. This explains why a family may be resistant to change, even when the members are saying or doing things to help one another on the surface.

Let's look at an example which incorporates all of the above. One family in therapy consists of a father, age 39; mother, age 38; sister, age 16; and brother age 14. The sister is considered "overweight," and doesn't like looking typically feminine. The family comes to therapy where the teenage daughter is the identified as the problem. The main complaint the parents express is "Sharon should lose weight, she should look softer and more feminine, she should find a boyfriend." During treatment, Sharon does manage to lose some weight. However, family members start keeping extra ice cream and cookies out in the open. Who is profiting here?

1. The billion dollar cosmetic industry that would make even more money if Sharon starting losing weight, wearing make-up, and trying to appear more like someone on a magazine cover instead of a healthy 16-year-old young woman.

2. Social norms, which have a vested interest in the status quo of keeping women's attention focused on their looks and their appearance so they will not utilize their intellectual and political power to their full potential.

3. The family system, in which members do not have to look at their own fears and worries as long as the sister continues to be the scapegoat for tensions.

No matter how you slice it, someone or something is profiting from any should which encourages you to buy something, think a certain way, or act in a way which results in feeling anxious or depressed. Remember this the next time you look in the mirror and pass judgment on yourself.

_____

_____

EXERCISE:

This exercise is intended to help you examine, "Who is profiting off my should?" Anytime you are shoulding yourself in some harmful way, there is someone who is profiting. Look back at your Should Pie. Is there anyone there who is profiting? Remember "profit" does not always mean something to do with money. Profit may be someone's investment in the status quo—in keeping things the same. Use the table below to consider how others may profit from your suffering. Include the should you've been writing about so far, but try thinking of others as well.

SHOULD CAUSING PAIN	WHO PROFITS OR GAINS FROM IT
[example]	
I should always be nice to everyone	My parents, my boss, my boyfriend
I should buy everyone gifts at the holidays	The toy corporations, the department stores

4. HOW DO I FEEL WHEN I THINK THIS SHOULD?

Honestly ask yourself this question without judgment. Do you feel anxious? Guilty about the past? Hopeless about the future? Sad? Depressed? Scared? Angry? Irritated? Frightened? Stressed?

Where in your body do you feel this should? Your shoulders? Your stomach? Your sides? Your forehead? All of us store feelings somewhere in our bodies. If you have experienced chronic aches and pains that a doctor cannot diagnose, then you know what I'm talking about. Excessive shoulds can result in poor digestion, fatigue, high blood pressure, ulcers, hypertension, and difficulty breathing. Do any of these sound familiar?

Now, recall the first line of this book—*Life doesn't have to be that hard.* There is an easier way to get through everyday living which allows more enjoyment, happiness, and peace. You have already begun this journey by reading this far. Read question #4 again and recognize what is implicit in this question—your feelings and emotions are a direct result of what you are thinking and believing. This concept was brought to the forefront of modern psychology by the great Dr. Albert Ellis in 1958 with the development of Rational Emotive Behavioral Therapy.

However, this concept was not new to the 20th century. Nearly 2000 years ago, the Greek philosopher Epictetus wrote that our emotions are determined by our perceptions: "Men are not disturbed by things, but by the view they take of them." Abraham Lincoln said, "Most folks are as happy as they make up their minds to be."

It is such a fundamental concept, and liberating when you think about it. Your frustration and everyday anxiety are not at the mercy of others. They are inside you, and therefore you have the ability to manage them and significantly reduce them. This statement, however, is entirely opposite to pretty much everything we learn in modern American culture. We are taught by consumerism to believe that our happiness and security are based on something or someone outside of us. We learn that we should purchase things in order to feel worth and meaning. We must obtain a product or a person or something external from ourselves to be whole. This conditioning absolves us from all responsibility in determining our own emotions, our own daily experience. If you have nothing to do with your moods, then of course you'll feel helpless, floundering, and stressed out!

By taking responsibility for your feelings, you take back your power. You are no longer like a leaf in a windstorm being thrashed from side to side. Now you are like a solid pole, anchored and steady. You are influenced by external factors, but not 100 percent determined by them. The world ceases to be quite so frightening and hopeless when you put yourself in charge of your thoughts and your actions.

> **CONSIDER THIS:**
>
> If you counted your shoulds as much as you counted your carbs, you would feel a lot healthier.

EXERCISE:

This exercise is intended to help answer the question, "How does it feel to think this 'should'?" It is very important to be aware of the feelings that arise when you decide to think these thoughts. Fill in the table below to help you become aware. You can use the same shoulds from the previous exercises, or write down some new ones that have come to mind since then.

THE SHOULD THOUGHT	THE FEELING
[example]	
I should lose some weight	unlovable, ugly, worthless
My boss shouldn't talk to me like that	angry, annoyed, inadequate
Prices should stop rising	angry, annoyed, inadequate

5. WHAT WOULD IT BE LIKE TO GO ONE DAY WITHOUT THIS SHOULD?

Imagine waking up and not having this Big Should hanging on you. To have one day when you have no should about what you should do, how you should do it, what you should wear, how you should look, how others should act, or how the world should be. Imagine one day in which, "I should lose some weight" never crosses your mind. If you're not concerned about your weight, go back to chapter 1 and imagine a day without one of the shoulds you checked off.

Most of us feel a tremendous sense of relief at this prospect. What is the first thing you would do in the morning? Who would you want to talk to? Where would you want to go? What would it be like? Relax, you don't have to act on it, just for now imagine it. Recognize what it's like to have a day without anxiety and stress.

_____

_____

_____

_____

_____

_____

_____

_____

_____

_____

_____

EXERCISE:

What would it feel like to go one day without this should? Often this is referred to as "The Miracle Question" in solution-focused treatments. Again, think about just one should that is causing you distress right now. List it below:

_____

_____

Now answer these questions:

Imagine you wake up one morning and that should is completely nonexistent for one day. What would it feel like to wake up on such a day?

_____

_____

_____

_____

_____

What is the first thing you would do?

_____

_____

_____

_____

_____

_____

List some other activities you would enjoy during the day.

_____
_____
_____
_____
_____
_____

Who would you want to do these activities with?

_____
_____
_____
_____
_____

Who would you try to talk to with whom you wouldn't ordinarily try to communicate?

_____
_____
_____
_____

How would it feel to live for one day in such a world without this should?

_____
_____
_____
_____
_____

6. WHO WOULD I BE WITHOUT THIS SHOULD?

This may seem like a peculiar question to ask yourself, but it moves toward important issues of identity. Many people have carried shoulds around with them for so long, they no longer have any idea who they are without them. Typically, these are individuals that perceive themselves as not living up to certain expectations.

Gwen, a 33-year-old woman, expressed the should we have been discussing: "I should lose weight." We explored the first six questions. She was able to recognize that she learned this should from a societal expectation. She recognized that this was a consequence of living in a society that valued her more for her waist size than for her mind. She was aware that this was not true for everyone everywhere 24/7, and that it was quite possible for some women to be attractive and feel good when carrying extra weight. She was aware that it was pharmaceutical companies and the magazine industry that profited off her should. She felt guilty and hopeless when she believed this should. When she thought about going one day without this should, an incredible sense of relief came over her.

"Still," she said after all this, "I feel like I should lose more weight."

Hmmm, is it possible to go through these questions and still feel miserable? It turns out that is an option if your Core Beliefs are at odds with feeling happy and empowered. Let's look at the above example with Gwen. Her inability to live up to her own should, and therefore to regularly fail, enables her to perceive herself as inherently inferior. In a case such as this, any inquiry about this or any other should will come into direct conflict with this Core Belief of being inadequate and being unlovable.

As discussed in chapter 2, "Core Beliefs" are like mental templates: they are the solid foundation upon which we form thoughts and judgments about ourselves. If there is a part of me that truly believes I'm unlovable, that I will be constantly thinking thoughts that support it. To demonstrate with Gwen:

I should lose weight +

I can't lose weight =

I'm a failure, I'm unlovable.

Gwen then gets caught in a cycle in which her shoulds are maintained and fueled by her Core Beliefs of being a failure and unlovable. She has no concept of who she is if she is not failing or imperfect. If she did lose weight, she would simply find another way to see herself in a harmful light.

If you also are finding that ideas in this book clash with internal Core Beliefs related to who you are, then I encourage you to seek out additional therapy or counseling. Find someone who is aware of cognitive-behavioral therapy, who can help you question the evidence for believing such devastating and inaccurate notions.

The good news is, just like all shoulds, you learned them at some point. None of us was born into this world believing, "I'm a loser and an all around terrible person." If you learned it, that means you can unlearn it.

_____

_____

_____

EXERCISE:

This exercise is intended to help you with the question, "Who would I be without this should?" Living without shoulds can be a wonderful experience. But it can also throw one's identity into flux. Use this exercise below to consider what making such a change could mean to you.

What are some of the adjectives you would use to describe yourself now?

_____

_____

_____

What are some of the adjectives you would use to describe yourself if you let go of the shoulds that are troubling you the most today?

_____

_____

_____

Look at the difference between these two. Which is preferable?

If the second response if preferable, congratulations, you are ready to make some major internal changes that will help you feel better overall in this world. You can skip the questions below.

But if the first response is preferable, you may be able to identify some secondary gain for staying upset. Remember, as discussed in chapter 2, secondary gain is not always obvious and not always intentional. But it can keep you stuck in being miserable.

What might be the secondary gain for staying upset?

_____

_____

_____

What would help you let go of this secondary gain?

_____

_____

_____

Who would be unhappy or angry if you let go of these shoulds in your life?

_____

_____

_____

Who would be happiest for you if you let go of these shoulds in your life?

_____

_____

_____

What are some of the drawbacks or disadvantages of change in your life?

_____

_____

_____

_____

_____

What are some of the advantages of change in your life?

_____

_____

_____

_____

_____

_____

_____

_____

_____

CHAPTER 3 **WHO SAYS I SHOULD?**

7. NOW REPLACE IT.

Don't forget this last crucial step. The way you use language will also directly impact your feelings, and your actions. The words you choose create and shape your beliefs and thoughts. If you use words to should yourself and others, you will continue to have all the undesirable feelings discussed in the previous section. By replacing should with a different phrase, you start to introduce freedom and choice to decide what kind of feeling you want to have. Here are some examples of words that can be used to replace *should*:

"could"	"prefer to"
"it would be beneficial to"	"choose to"
"it would be healthy to"	"it would demonstrate respect to"

Try saying, "I prefer to lose weight, but I am lovable no matter what." "I could lose weight." "It might be beneficial physically if I lost weight." "I could honor love I have for myself and for the people who care about me by losing weight." How does that feel?

Some self-help programs recommend that you simply need to change a "negative" statement into a "positive" in order to feel better. My only qualm with this is that if you don't back up your words with belief and conviction, then they don't hold very much meaning. When you state, "I prefer to lose weight but I am lovable no matter what" after going through the six questions, you say it with intelligence and rationality, knowing that anyone who disagrees has an agenda to benefit or profit from you somehow. You know that it's possible that such a statement may conflict with a harmful Core Belief, but you can seek additional treatment if you have trouble letting go of it. And when you do, you will be in a position to utilize the power of your knowledge to have a much easier day.

EXERCISE:

There are many ways to replace "should" with other terms that are less demanding, less fearful, and bring more hope and empowerment. Using the tools you now have available to you from this book, try finding some replacements to the shoulds that you have listed in previous exercises.

_____

_____

_____

_____

_____

_____

_____

_____

CONSIDER THIS:

If you spent as much time working on your shoulds as you did working out at the gym, you would feel a lot happier.

CHAPTER 4
REAL PEOPLE VERSUS THEIR SHOULDS –
ROGER'S ROAD RAGE, ROSA'S CHRISTMAS GUILT

Now let's examine some examples of how one can practice living *absolutely should-less* in everyday situations. These excerpts are based on actual sessions I have had with clients. Names have been changed, and most of the people are composites of several individuals I have had the privilege to work with in counseling sessions.

Roger is a 34-year-old male, struggling with issues related to stress, anger management, depression, and substance abuse.

Roger ("R"): So I'm driving along to get here on time, and this jerk completely cuts me off. He's comes up on the back of me, you know, like he's going to hit me, then pulls in front of me, then he slows down! Now why do that? I'm telling you, this is one of those times I'm glad I don't carry a gun with me because in that very moment I felt it.

Damon ("D"): Felt it?

R: Yeah, the boiling point. That point where you are just ready to go off, and damn the consequences. I would have blown off his smug little head, see how he would have felt then.

D: What would you say to him if you could?

R: That you shouldn't do that, man, you shouldn't cut people off like that, it's wrong. It's dangerous. Especially if someone shoots you, because I'll tell you, not everyone is as civilized as I am.

D: So Roger, I'm hearing a lot of anger in what you're feeling today, would you say that is correct?

R: Yeah, I'm angry, people shouldn't drive like that!

D: On a scale of 1-10, with 10 being the angriest you ever get, how angry do you feel now as you're talking to me about it?

R: When I tell you about it, when I see that smug guy's face, I'd say I'm at a 9.2.

D: Okay, that's pretty high. Now Roger, I want to ask you honestly, would you like to bring that number down a bit? Are you willing?

R: Yeah, well, that's why I'm here. Right, I want to learn how to handle this better. I sometimes get so angry, so upset, I do things I regret later. I don't want to always fly off the handle.

D: Well, what happened today I think provides an opportunity for you to practice control over your reaction, control of your actions. The main problem I am seeing here is not that this stranger cut you off, it is your reaction to it. It is the thought behind it that you have shared, "He *shouldn't* have cut me off like that." I want to ask you some questions now and see if you feel better afterward. Can we try that?

R: Sure, I'm willing.

D: Okay. First of all Roger, how did you learn that this guy shouldn't have cut you off?

R: How did I learn? I learned it from the DMV first of all. Then, well, my father taught me to drive. And I've told you about him, he's the kind of guy who actually would threaten to shoot someone who cut him off on the road. He would never take that crap from anyone.

D: Great, who else?

R: Well, like you've said in weeks before, the society we live in. It sets up rules which say "you should not do stupid stuff that puts other people's lives at risk." Maybe not exactly like that, but it's implied with the laws we have about driving and following rules. Society says that people shouldn't act that way. It's even the law!

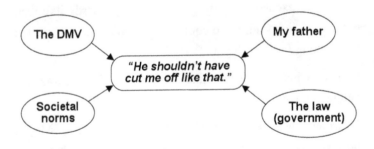

D: Okay, Roger, now let me ask you this: is this true for everyone everywhere 24/7? Can you ever see a good reason why someone might do that?

R: To cut someone off, like what?

D: Well, you tell me, have you ever cut someone off?

R: Well, yeah, I've done it, but I had a good reason. My girlfriend at the time called me, she was feeling really sick, she wanted me to come over, she was like howling in pain and didn't want to call a doctor or anything. So I'm rushing to get to her place, and was behind this really slow driver. I pulled ahead of her, but then a dog was running onto the road and I had to swerve and break fast. It's amazing I didn't get hit that time.

D: Yeah, it is amazing. Now from the other driver's point of view, what happened?

R: (laughs) Well, from her point of view, it was probably like, "some ass cut me off and then put on the brakes really fast."

D: Aha! So there is a time and place when cutting off someone may not be an act of rudeness or aggression.

R: Well, it wasn't when I did it. But that wasn't the case today.

D: How do you know? I mean just for argument sake, how do you know what was going on? Maybe the guy had a reason. There's no excuse for putting someone in jeopardy like that, but as you just said, there could be an explanation for it that has nothing to do with you.

R: I see what you mean. Like maybe his girlfriend was sick and that's why he was rushing.

D: Maybe. Maybe someone he knew was in trouble. Maybe he was having a medical problem. Whatever the case is, I think we can agree that this notion that "this person shouldn't have cut me off" may not apply to everyone everywhere 24/7, is this true?

R: Maybe not. I guess there are times someone may have a legitimate reason for doing it. I have no idea if that was the case here, but I guess just thinking about that makes me feel less like blowing someone's head off.

D: Well, that's something then, isn't it? So, my next question for you, Roger, is, who is profiting from your should?

R: Profiting from it? Like how?

D: Let me put it like this: When your anger goes up to a 9.2, what happens to your body?

R: Oh, well, I know it's not good. My blood pressure goes up, that's for sure. When I'm really angry, I feel like there's a hole burning in my stomach. I get all worked up, and then I really want a nice cold beer to calm me down. I don't sleep so well either.

D: Ah, so high blood pressure, stomach pains, craving for alcohol, and insomnia. Let me ask you again, Roger, who is profiting then off your should about the way others drive?

R: I guess the doctors who I'm going to have to see if I keep my blood pressure up. The people who make Tums to settle my stomach. Certainly the people who make and sell beer have made a pretty penny off my anger. The company that makes sleeping medicines also does well off of me.

D: So there are a lot of businesses that are making cash off of your suffering, is that right?

R: Yeah, well, yeah. They're sitting there counting their cash while I get upset and angry. That doesn't really seem fair.

D: No, it doesn't. So Roger, so far we've established that you learned early on from various sources that drivers shouldn't cut you off, you come to realize that this may not be true 100% of the time, and you've identified that thinking this "should" sends your anger up to a 9.2, and then you've told me about all the companies who make money from you when your anger soars. You with me so far?

R: I'm with you. I'm just sitting here still thinking of all the people who profit off my thinking a certain way.

D: It's true, there are industries invested in your suffering. As you mentioned, society sets it up for you to judge others in a narrow rigid way. Then, when people act differently from how you think they should, it naturally upsets you. When you get upset, you...

R: ...spend money to try to feel better. Okay. So then what you're saying is, the way out of this is not to try to make others act the way I want them to, it's to change the way I react to how they're acting?

D: Exactly, Roger, that's very well put. It is not that driver that made you angry, it is your should about his driving that made you angry. And that should is something that is in your control. Let's try this: Take a deep breath, and tell me what it would be like to wake up and for one day not have any shoulds about other people's driving?

R: One day? Well that would be a better day. I could just get from point A to point B without honking, without clenching my teeth, without getting so pissed. That would be good.

D: And who would you be if you didn't have shoulds about the way other people drive?

R: I would be a lot more relaxed, a lot more accepting, probably an easier person to be around.

D: Now instead of "people shouldn't cut me off," can you think of any other way to say that?

R: Maybe, "I don't want people to cut me off," or, "I wish people didn't cut me off."

D: What would it be like to say, "I'd prefer people would drive the right way, but I'm going to stay calm regardless of what they do."

R: That works for me, I like that.

D: And thinking about that now here with me, how angry do you feel?

R: Right now? I don't feel angry at all, maybe like a "1" at the most.

D: Only a "1"? How did you get from a "9.2" to "1" in such a short period of time?

R: Well, I'm not driving right now (laughs).

D: True, you're not in the immediate situation, but you weren't when you first came in here either. What has changed?

R: Well, I'm thinking about it differently now.

D: And how does thinking about it differently change things?

R: It doesn't change things at all, but it changes me. I know when I go back out there I may be surrounded by stupid drivers again. But I'm beginning to realize that I have a choice. To go nuts with anger. Or, to recognize that people may have reasons for doing things that I don't understand, I don't have to make myself angry and upset just because other people do stupid things. All I need to do is pay attention and make sure I don't get hurt on the road.

D: Exactly, Roger, you've perfectly identified the crux of these questions—*you can't change what other people do, but you can change your reaction to it.* And there is the beginning of being that relaxed person you would like to be. You can apply this same line of thinking to any situation you're in where people appear to be acting differently from how you want them to. You never have to give them the power to ruin your whole day, to cause you total pain.

Roger illustrated a problem that most of us experience, especially while driving: I know how other people should behave. As Roger realized, believing in this should was a one way ticket to his doctor's office or the nearest bar, which ever was closer. For many others road rage leads to jail, the hospital, or even the morgue. He came to understand that trying to control the way other people act was futile and would only hurt him. Even if you're not driving, any time you try to use should to control what other people say or do, you are traveling down the same road.

Rosa is a 36-year-old single mother of four coping with a family history of major depression, and herself with past issues with cocaine abuse. She struggles to be financially independent by accepting welfare and taking some cleaning jobs on the side. This conversation took place during the last week of November.

Damon (D): So what's going on today, Rosa? You seem pretty down.

Rosa (R): Yes, you know, the holidays are here again. You know what that means.

D: Well, I'm not sure what they mean to you. Can you tell me more?

R: It's just...you know...(starts crying), here's the thing. I'm trying, you know, sometimes I fall behind, most of the time I do alright. But then around this time of year, the kids see toys on TV, toys in the windows, they look up at me and say, "That's what I want, Mommy."

D: Have you considered explaining to them what the situation is this year or maybe encouraging them to save their own money?

R: I try, Damon, really I do. It's just when I look in their faces, in their eyes, and see the disappointment, I just feel like I'm the worse parent ever. I should be able to get them those toys, I should be able to buy them anything they want for Christmas. All of their friends are talking about what they think they're gonna get. I should be able to get my kids the same things, anything they want.

D: Rosa, it seems that this should about buying them whatever they want for Christmas is bringing you a lot of pain today. Is that fair to say?

R: Yes, absolutely, I'd say so.

D: So could we explore that a bit more, just some of the thoughts around that?

R: Sure, O.K.

D: Now, first of all let's pinpoint one of the shoulds going on—"I should be able to buy my kids anything they want for Christmas." How did you learn that should?

R: I'm not sure I know what you mean.

D: Let me put it like this. None of us popped out of the womb saying, "Hey, when I'm a parent I should be able to buy my kids anything I want for Christmas," right?

R: Right, O.K.

D: So somewhere along the way you learned this to be true. How did you learn it?

R: Well, I start thinking about my parents. Even though they couldn't give us everything we wanted, I know they wanted to. I know they tried. Let's see. Well, definitely the TV.

D: How does TV influence this should?

R: Look at the messages out there! They're always showing kids happy enjoying these toys. And then they're saying,

"You should buy more and your kids will be happy. If you don't you're a crappy parent." Something like that.

D: Great, so TV and merchandising really affect your feelings about yourself as a parent. Who else?

R: Well, my kids themselves. They either see it on TV or talk about it in school and then they're like, "Mommy, mommy, so and so is getting this, I want it too." That hurts so much, it really does.

D: So TV and you own kids are affecting your shoulds and how you feel about yourself. What else?

R: Um, I guess the environment too.

D: Say more?

R: Well, where we live. Everyone knows everyone's business at these places, I'm telling you. Everyone knows what everyone is doing, and everyone knows who gets what for Christmas. When I hear about some people giving their kids more presents than I give mine, that makes it even worse. I feel even worse.

D: I see, so it sounds like there's almost a comparison competition thing happening. Christmas becomes a time to show each other up, to try to see who can out do the others?

R: (laughs) It sounds ridiculous, doesn't it? But it's true. I wish it wasn't that way.

D: Well the good news, Rosa, is that it doesn't have to be that way. It's true that you can't control what your kids see and talk about, and how other people see you and judge you. But you <u>can</u> assert energy in not allowing all that to hurt you 100% of the time. Let's go forward and see if we can make that happen together, okay?

R: Okay.

D: Now, tell me Rosa, is it true that everyone everywhere should be able to buy their kids whatever they want for Christmas every year?

R: No, I don't think so.

D: Okay, why not?

R: Well, (laughs) maybe the kids don't deserve it. Um, it's not true, because parents can't always afford to buy their kids everything they want. And if they do, they may sacrifice other things, like clothes for the winter, food, school supplies, the ability to do other things for birthdays and stuff. (pauses) And if I gave them everything they wanted, that would be the case. I wouldn't have money for anything else. Not even rent.

D: So for real, what do your children really need?

R: They need food, they need a roof, they need clothes. They need light so they can do their homework, they need a mother who is there and sober.

D: And in this past year, haven't you given your children all those things?

R: Yes (tearful), I have. (pause) So maybe I'm not such a bad parent after all.

D: I'd go along with that. I'd also say you just brilliantly answered the question. It's not true everyone everywhere should give their children everything they want for Christmas. And it's not true for you either, is it?

R: No.

D: But when you think that thought, how does it feel?

R: It hurts, it makes it seem like I'm not good enough.

D: And when you think of all the ways you have provided for you children this year, how hard you have fought to stay clean, and how you have given them the true gift of having a sober mother, how does that feel?

R: That feels good, I'm really proud of that.

D: And what you can see illustrated right here, Rosa, is how you have the power to change your feelings anytime you need to. Again, you can't control what others say and do, but you can assert control with how you take it in. You always have the option to use the power of your thoughts to focus on all the destructive shoulds that hurt you. Or, you can think thoughts that are more accurate—that you are doing a great job as a parent, giving those kids what they truly need. Unfortunately, Christmas is a time of year when certain people feel a need to try to put you down and hurt you for their own financial gain. Can we talk about that for a few minutes?

R: Sure.

D: O.K., anytime you're having the thought, "I should be able to buy my kids whatever they want for Christmas," there is someone profiting. Can you imagine who is profiting off your shoulds, who is profiting from your pain?

R: I suppose it would be whoever is taking the money that I spend when I feel guilty.

D: I'd say so. Who is that?

R: Well, probably the greedy toy companies. And then there's the department stores that carry it, the people who work there, the factories that ship the toys, the TV stations that play the commercials, the corporations who sponsor them. A lot of people!

D: Now you get it. When you put it like that, Rosa, doesn't it makes sense that all these people have a vested interest in getting your money any way they can? They must, or they wouldn't have jobs. And through lots of research, they have found that the best way to make money and keep their jobs secure is to try to make you, the working parent, feel guilty. They assume that if you feel guilty, you'll spend money to try to feel good. And most of the time they're right! It's not that all these people are "evil..."

R: No, they're just trying to do what they have to do.

D: Right. The point of all this is that there is a multibillion-dollar industry built upon you feeling like you should be able to give you children anything they want for Christmas. And you have the choice not to give them the satisfaction. Every time you feel like you should be a better parent, someone is profiting. That's where you assert choice. Now, I want you to try to imagine one day, just one day, in which you wake up in the morning, and there is no should saying you should be able to buy your children anything they want for Christmas. Can you imagine that?

R: (smiling, appearing visibly more relaxed), Oh my God, that would be a great day. That just feels like such a relief! Like I can let all that go. Like I'm free. It's so different, I never really realized what I was doing to myself.

D: Yes, just focus on how good it feels to live life without this should. You can have that anytime you want. It may be harder to do it out there than it is in here, but you have the ability to at least reduce the impact those shoulds have on you, and feel this relief more frequently.

R: I like that.

D: Now, one more question, Rosa. I want you be in the moment of feeling good, and think honestly, who would you be without this should? If you never had this weighing on you, would would you be?

R: Wow, I don't even know, I'm not even sure.

D: Do you think you'd still be able to think of yourself as such a bad parent?

R: No, absolutely not. When I feel like this, I think I'm a good parent. I may not be perfect, but I've worked hard and I'm doing my best. Even with all the things I've done wrong, those kids have never once gone hungry. I'm there as much as I can be, which is more than a lot of other parents. I've never shortchanged them with love no matter what. So maybe we'll just get through this thing, and even if it's hard, I won't forget that I am a good parent. I won't forget I do my best no matter what.

Rosa's session again highlights many ideas discussed in previous chapters. She demonstrates how one's mood can be shifted by altering one's perception. In this case, her thought, "I should be able to buy my children anything they want for Christmas" was masking an underlying core belief, "I'm a bad parent." As you can see, in this case the questions were not asked in order. There are no shoulds about asking the questions in any kind of order, just what seems to flow best.

CONSIDER THIS:

If you spent as much as time watching your shoulds as you did the stock market, you would end up a lot richer (emotionally, anyway!)

CHAPTER 5
YES, BUT...

As you have been reading, I'm sure you have had your reservations. After all, some of these concepts at first may appear to run contrary to common sense. It is natural to resist new ideas, especially those which challenge the fabric of your earliest teachings. The prospect of truly living life joyfully without shoulds brings up intense fears in some people. Many picture a world of anarchy and chaos that could arise without such rigid rules and standards. But what I am proposing would result in just the opposite.

Some have said to me, "If I didn't have shoulds, why would I go to work? Why would I stay sober? Why would I practice safe sex? Why would I take my medicines? Why would I get exercise? Quit smoking? Take a shower? Get out of bed at all?"

Indeed, why would you? Think about it for a moment: why would you do any of these things now? Then let's follow this line of thinking rationally. You may go to work day to day without necessarily feeling like you want to, but knowing that a consequence of not going to work would be losing a paycheck. Then, if you lost a paycheck, what would happen next? You may not be able to buy as much food for yourself or someone you love. You may not be able to afford clothing. Perhaps you wouldn't be able to pay heating or electric bills. You could lose your home if you didn't pay your rent or mortgage. By going to work, even when you don't want to, you are prioritizing these needs for yourself and those you love.

"So," you may say, "how is this different from what I do now? I wake up in the morning and would so much rather go to the movies than to my crummy job. Like you said, if I don't go, there will be hell to pay. Therefore, I should go!"

No, this is where we would disagree. "Should" implies you are doing something specifically because you are afraid of the consequences. It is a motivator fundamentally based in fear of future events. It may have some immediate benefits in the short term, but in the long term is more likely to cause resentment, burnout, and inconsistency.

Conversely, you can make choices to do things you don't feel like doing because you choose to demonstrate love and respect for yourself, and those around you, in the here and now. Instead of saying "I should go to work today," try replacing it with "I could go to work today," or "I choose to go to work today," or, "I choose to demonstrate love for myself and my family by going to work today."

Just notice the difference in how it feels to speak these phrases out loud. Start with a more benign task, such as, cleaning your house. Say:

"I should clean the house this weekend."

Notice how it feels to say that. Then, try replacing "should" with another phrase. Some examples might be:

"I could clean the house this weekend."

"It would feel good to have a clean house."

"I choose to demonstrate honor and respect for myself and others by cleaning the house this weekend."

Did you feel a difference? If you're one of those people who actually likes to clean the house on occasions, then try substituting this with a task you ordinarily would not enjoy.

Now try this with a bigger task. Many people who have to take medicine every day, for either physical or psychiatric reasons, have a lot of negative feelings about this. They may have an attitude like, "I shouldn't have to take these medications every day," "I shouldn't be sick," "I shouldn't have to be different from other people." Such thoughts quite often result in people missing doses, and thereby compromising the effectiveness of the medications that have been prescribed.

Try saying every negative thing you can think of about taking medications. About how intrusive they are, about the side effects, all the reasons that you shouldn't have to take them. Then, try honestly saying to yourself, "I choose to take medications because they can help me get better. I prefer to demonstrate love for myself and for those around me by taking the drugs the way they have been prescribed. I could tell my doctor about any uncomfortable side effects so that I may have an easier time taking them." Again, notice the difference in how this now feels.

Safer sex is also an area where fear is frequently used to promote a certain behavior. For over 25 years, HIV educators have tried to use fear and shoulds to motivate people to use condoms more frequently, with varied results. Why is this? If people know how HIV is spread, and if they know it can kill you, why wouldn't it follow suit that they would always use condoms 100 percent of the time?

As we have said before, how motivated do *you* feel when you are told you should do anything? Yes, scaring people about HIV has found to be a short term motivator in the fight against spreading the virus. But in the long-term, shoulds have not been found to sustain healthy behavior patterns. This holds just as true for antismoking campaigns and anti-drug messages, and other such instances in which educators continue to ponder how and why individuals would engage in self-destructive behavior patterns knowing all the facts. Why don't they work? Because *shoulds do not change the beliefs or thoughts that created* the problematic behavior in the first place. If I do not value my body as deserving of happiness and health, it won't matter what shoulds someone is address-ing toward me, I will still abuse it with drugs and unsafe sex.

When educators and authorities teach others that they "can" make healthier choices, when they explore options as possibly valid "preferences," then they start to create internal-ized motivation to act less self-destructive. More clearly, when it is demonstrated to people that they can make choices that are fundamentally based in love and respect, as opposed to fear and shame, then the likelihood that someone will take posi-tive steps consistently is increased. Reframing these choices may include saying, "I decide not to abuse drugs," "I choose to prioritize my health and therefore use condoms with sex," "I choose to quit smoking not because I should, but out of a sense of honor for me, for my body, and for those who love me." All involve changing perception first, behaviors second.

Many employers mistakenly operate under the guise that they can increase productivity by telling their employees that they should work harder, better, or more effectively. Once again, when has this ever worked? Do you honestly feel like working harder when your boss says you "should" ? Or do you feel like complying on the surface just to get him/her off your back, and then going back to doing things your own way? I have worked in many clinics where supervisors have told employees how they should accomplish goals, and then genuinely seem perplexed when these projects are not carried out that way. Again, when one uses shame and fear to control behavior, it rarely has any lasting impact.

Shoulds do not increase long-term healthy choices and priorities. When I think of taking action because I should, I imagine a car getting pushed down a steep hill with the emergency brake on. True, eventually that car will get to the bottom of that hill. But imagine what kind of shape it will be in by that point. It will be torn, tattered, burnt out. The same applies to us if we go through our lives taking action from a place of should. Yes, you may get to work on time. Yes, that house might get clean. But what kind of shape will you be in emotionally or physically by that point? Remember, the first sentence of this book: Life doesn't have to be that hard. It is quite possible to be a happy, healthy, valuable member of your community, and not suffer quite so much. It is possible to make choices from a place of love instead of fear. Try it, and you will notice the difference.

"Yes," you might say, "but the way I feel isn't always that rational. I may know it's okay to gain a few pounds, but still may feel lousy about it. Are you saying I shouldn't feel bad about this?"

Nothing of the sort. I have no right to tell anyone on this earth how they should feel, and neither do you! You have a right to feel as lousy as you wish, and there may be valid secondary gain for continuing to be miserable (see chapter 2).

At the same time, sometimes feeling lousy doesn't feel like a choice at all. Using a rational approach to reduce suffering doesn't always provide immediate relief. But much like working a muscle in your body, the more you do it, the more effective it becomes. The more you pay attention to the thoughts that bring you suffering and the thoughts that bring you joy and peace, the more you will become aware of how to change your mind to improve your mood.

"Yes, but there are things bringing me pain that I shouldn't have to be feeling. My partner and I are ending a long term relationship. I may have to move. My dog just died. I feel sad almost every minute of every day. How does being absolutely should-less apply to this?"

Keep in mind, there is nothing wrong with feeling sadness, grief, anger, or remorse. These are healthy and normal parts of living life and loving others. It's when you tell yourself that you "shouldn't" be having these feelings that you can get into trouble. When you judge and should your emotions and reactions, you are just adding to the misery you already feel.

Imagine that a boyfriend or girlfriend breaks up with you. That, by itself, can be an extremely painful event. But what happens when you tell yourself, "I shouldn't feel so bad about this." That feels worse! It is only natural then to want to escape from feeling so terrible. Drug and alcohol abuse is one such self destructive action that is a consequence of telling yourself such cruel shoulds. Notice how often you should yourself about your own feelings. Do you really feel better afterwards?

"Yes, but I'm a supervisor at my job who is responsible for making sure people do things the right way. If they don't do it right, we don't get paid. Why wouldn't you use 'should' then?"

Because by telling other people how they should do something, you are not instilling any long term motivation to do it effectively. Should simply inspires one to agree with you, and then either forget to do it that way or do it their own way if they think they won't get caught. Consider the adage, "Give a man a fish, he'll eat for a day. Teach a man to fish, he'll never go hungry again." I would add, "Give an employee a should, they'll work your way for a day. Teach them why a task has to be done, and they'll never mess up again." Instead of telling someone, "You should fill out that form like this," try saying, "Forms have to be filled out this way in order to comply with our licensing agency," or "The business needs you to do this form in a certain way in order to stay vital and continue to pay your salary." Spoken with genuine respect, this can make a huge difference in the performance of your employees.

"But hey, there are some shoulds I have that are right! People shouldn't abuse children! They shouldn't keep raising my clinic fees! People should be nice to each other! There shouldn't be any war! Gas prices shouldn't keep rising! How can you disagree with these ideas?"

Remember, I'm not agreeing or disagreeing with any of these ideas; they are between you and your own principles. What is problematic is the repercussions from insisting that your should is absolutely right. I am concerned with how your should is affecting your emotional and physical health.

For example, let's take a fairly common societal belief: People should not talk on cell phones during movies. Most, though clearly not all, people believe this, some pretty strongly. Many make the case, "It's rude, it's insensitive. If I pay that much for a movie, I want to enjoy it in peace and quiet." Fair enough. But when you demand how right you are, this is when we start getting into trouble.

Next time you find yourself shoulding someone else's behavior, try to ask these questions: How does it feel to be so right? Do you get angry? Do you get an adrenaline rush? Do you get so frustrated you just decide never to do it again? Do you get upset that others don't see the world the way you do? Do you have trouble sleeping when others do things you think they shouldn't? What does being so right do to your blood pressure? To your neck? To your stomach? For most people, such insistence on being right has an adverse reaction on all these levels, thereby increasing the possibility of ulcers, heart disease, or high blood pressure.

But it's also costing you on an emotional level. When you are sitting there during your movie, and someone is answering his cell phone, and you just know how right you are that he shouldn't be doing that, how does that honestly feel? For most people, this sense of being right creates anger, resentment, and often a sense of powerlessness and hopelessness. They may think, "Why bother trying to do anything or have any fun if nobody acts the way I think they should? What difference do my beliefs make? If the world is going to hell anyway, what's the point? I might as well kick that guy's ass!"

Clearly there are some pretty devastating ramifications to having to be "right." These are shoulds that often compromise your ability to respond clearly. They may lead to violent crimes, legal entanglements, or at the very least, many visits to the doctors and to therapists. Yet most of us experience these shoulds on some level every day, either at work, at home, in traffic, at the gym, or in any social situation. Unfortunately, other people are simply never always going to do what you think they should do!

So if you get nothing else from this book, get this: There are times you will have to choose between being right and being happy. Ideally it would not be this way, and we would all be able to coexist happily and peacefully. But we are humans, we are different, and we all have different precise ideas of how others humans, from our parents to politicians to the shlub in the movie theater, should act. Others may agree with you, but they won't have the ulcers for you. You do have a choice in these situations. You can choose to suffer, or you can choose to live a happier more joy-filled life. If you choose the latter, read on!

CHAPTER 6
REAL PEOPLE VERSUS THEIR SHOULDS –
LENORE'S BODY IMAGE, MARK'S MANHOOD MYTH

L enore presents another example in which a person perceives herself as the "problem," and can gain much relief and happiness by changing her shoulds. Lenore is a 27-year-old African-American woman who is struggling with issues related to her weight. Although her doctor says she is of average weight given her height and family history, she sees her self otherwise:

Lenore (L): I don't like the way I look. I should lose weight. I should be thin.

Damon (D): Really, why?

L: Because it's disgusting to be fat, I see what's happening to me, I don't like it.

D: Okay, Lenore, how do you feel when say "I should be thin?"

L: I feel anxious, I feel stressed. I have tried so many diets, so many fads, you know, it just hasn't happened. I feel like I'm just hopeless.

D: And are you willing to investigate this with me, for the purpose of helping you feel better and less helpless and stressed?

L: Sure, if you think it will help.

D: I think it could. So Lenore, let me begin by saying that none of us came into this world stating, "I'm here, world, get me on the right diet so I can lose weight!" Kids don't worry about this until they learn otherwise. Can you think back and try to remember how you learned that you should be thin at such a young age?

L: In my family it was almost the opposite idea. I grew up in the South, and there was always plenty of food to go around. Especially on Sundays when the family and neighbors would come together. Food was just a part of that, and as a child I don't remember anyone saying, "careful what you eat."

D: So where do you think you learned it?

L: Well, actually, now I do remember there being a neighborhood boy who would call me "porky" or something like that. That's the first memory I have of looking at myself thinking I should look different. Then, in 7th grade, my family moving to New York, going through puberty, it was different. Girls were a lot more body conscious and judgmental here. I remember being around girls, black and white, who were skinny, who let me know one way or another it was not cool to be fat.

D: So here on the Should Pie we're getting a picture of how you learned the idea "I should be thin." Certain peers when you were young. Then your peers in adolescence. How about your family?

L: No, my family, my brothers didn't really say much about it. But I'll tell you what else I think mattered. Watching MTV as a kid. I'd see those girls in the videos, strutting around in lingerie with smoke flying everywhere, looking happy, sexy, important. I remember thinking, "I want to be like that, but that ain't never gonna happen in this chubby body."

D: Okay, so you're aware that the media, the television played a major role in forming this should which is causing you stress and misery now. What else?

L: Well, I mean, where I work now, the office I'm in, the girls are constantly talking about this diet, that diet, "I lost this many pounds," and I don't think they're going about it the best way either.

D: Aha, so coworkers are playing a role in this too. Who else?

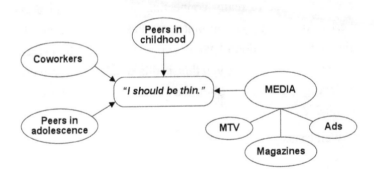

L: Um, well, I mean, just look at the magazines out there. Even on the subway coming down here I saw this ad for beer with this black girl looking skinny, happy, powerful, like if you want to be happy you have to look like that.

D: Exactly! So when we say media, we're including TV, magazines, advertisements, movies, pretty much every image out there, right?

L: Yeah I guess so, if you pay attention to it, it's out there, it can get to you.

D: Actually, Lenore, I'd say it's worse if you're not paying attention to it. At least you're aware and connecting how these images impact your shoulds. A lot of people are affected by them but don't even realize how constant exposure to these images shape their harmful shoulds every day. The images are always there and often are planned to be subtle so you don't consciously notice them, but certainly get hurt by them.

L: Well, I'm used to that. As a girl I noticed that it was always white women in these ads, that you rarely ever saw a beautiful black woman being used to sell things. Now you see it all the time, but they're impossibly thin and look like they're trying to look white. I'm not sure which is worse.

D: I'm not sure either. But I think what's really important here is that you're really connecting how media and peers overlap in giving you constant messages that you should be thin, and that you don't have to subscribe to that 100 percent of the time. Let me ask you this, is this should true for everyone everywhere 24/7? Should all women all over the world be thin?

L: Well (pause), maybe...no.

D: Why not?

L: Well, OK, let me put it like this. There are some men who like their ladies with "back," you know what I mean?

D: I believe so.

L: And I don't discriminate when it comes to men. Black, white, it doesn't matter to me. But I know enough to know that there are lots of men, brothers, who like their women with a little more meat. And, you know, I don't think women are expected to be this thin everywhere in the world.

D: Can you say more?

L: Well, I mean, this drive, this pressure to be like a skinny toothpick: you don't find that everywhere in the world. I went to Europe once in college, and lots of the beautiful women there looked like they had curves, and didn't seem to mind, you know? Even an ad I saw for skin lotion in a magazine just had this normal looking woman with some extra pounds on her who seemed healthy and happy.

D: Right! I think the United States is actually unusual in this way. The standards set for women are impossible for most to obtain without seriously hurting themselves. Yet if you looked at TV or movies, that's pretty much all you ever see. And as you said, it's not like this in all parts of the world. So if it's not true for them, why is it completely true for you?

L: O.K., I think I understand what you're saying. If women can be beautiful and happy in other parts of the world with some extra weight on them, why can't I have that here?

D: You've got it. So while we're talking about this, who do you think is profiting from your "should"?

L: Excuse me?

D: In other words, who gains from this, who has an interest in making you believe that you should be thin?

L: I suppose that beer company on the subway would be pretty happy to know they got to me. Which is ironic if you think about it—how do you stay thin if you drink so much beer?

D: Exactly! They put those ads to get to you, to reinforce the should that you should be thin. They're hoping that in the ensuing hopelessness and despair that you will buy more products to make yourself feel better. The diet industry spends billions of dollars banking on the fact that you will feel ashamed of your body in its natural state. MTV and the movies you see feed into that by only presenting images of women who are very thin—all with the intended result of getting you to invest in your own harmful shoulds, and then spend more money.

L: That sounds like such a conspiracy when you put it like that.

D: I wouldn't say "conspiracy" so much as I'd say "industry." These are corporations we are talking about. They are CEOs sitting in offices, and they have children to send through college. They are banking on you believing there is something wrong with who you are.

L: So when I doubt myself, I'm just playing into the Man's hands?

D: It sure would seem that way. Now let's look again at some of these movies and TV shows. We already established that you rarely ever see a healthy looking woman with "back" on these shows. But when you look at the men, what do you see?

L: Well, for men, it's different. You can look at TV shows, see fat guys with young skinny wives, but you never see the opposite.

D: And why do you think that is?

L: Because they think that's what men want to see?

D: More than that. I would go so far to say that the absence of women over 40 and exclusion of women of a normal size is a symptom of a much larger issue. That is, how misogyny, a hatred of women, plays out in our culture. Men don't have the same pressures that women do. We do get some, but we're not told we should be thin constantly to the same degree that women do. There are representations of men as you pointed out in the media. Old, young, thin, fat. But the question comes back to this: who else is profiting off your thought that you should be thin?

L: I guess in that way, any man who doesn't like women. They want us to be more concerned with our weight and appearance than they do our reproductive rights and how unfair it is we make less money and things like that. Men suck, no offense.

D: None taken.

L: So why should I? I mean, why would I believe the hype that I need to be thin if it's just keeping all that going? Why would anyone?

D: Good point. But as you've pointed out, these messages are so insidious, most of us are usually not even aware they're being directed at us when it's happening.

L: Okay, that's true, but what if I just want to be thin on my own? With no shoulds attached, but just because it feels better or my doctor says it's healthier?

D: Then I'd say if you're making a choice that's coming from an honest place within yourself of wanting to feel healthier, and if it's stemming from a place of love for yourself and your body instead of fear, then you will absolutely make that happen. You will then have the internal motivation to really sustain a consistent healthy regimen that allows you to meet your goals. But when you say to yourself, "I should be thin," how does that feel?

L: Like I said before, it feels stressful. It feels hopeless, pretty lousy.

D: And when you say to yourself, "I could lose weight," how does that feel?

L: It's only a change of one word, but it feels better. Like I want it to happen but I'm okay either way.

D: You get it! The beliefs behind "should" and "could" are completely different. With "should" you're saying it had better happen or else. With "could" you express a preference. A preference is far easier and more enjoyable to work with than a rigid standard. Shoulds sometimes can produce some results in the short term as far as weight loss, but I have never seen someone sustain that momentum when their primary motivation is shame or fear. You always have a choice to say "I could lose weight," or "I could demonstrate love for myself and those who love me by taking care of myself and eating better, but either way I'm a beautiful deserving person."

L: I like that, I'm going to try that.

D: What would one day be like without the thought, "I should be thin?"

L: Oh, Lord, that would just be marvelous. I'm starting to feel now how that could be.

D: And one more question, Lenore. Who would you be without this thought?

L: What do you mean?

D: Quite often, we get into patterns of identifying with our shoulds. I'll ask someone, "Who are you," and they'll say, "I'm the screw-up who can't lose weight." When you've carried this should for so long, it can become part of your identity, your internal core beliefs about who you are.

L: Like who would I be if I didn't see myself as wrong?

D: Yes. Who?

L: (pause) I guess I'd actually have to see myself as lovable. If I totally believed I was alright no matter what I weighed, I'd have to see myself as a loving gorgeous woman.

Lenore started the session fairly upset by her thoughts that she should be thin. Once she could locate that should in its cultural and political context, she felt more control over it. This is not to say that the thought never bothered her again. However, she now has a frame of reference for making herself feeling better, and communicating with other women about her struggles

In the case of Mark, a 49-year-old accountant, we once again see how shoulds within oneself, and in a relationship, can affect depression. Mark has been married to his wife Kerry for the past seven years:

Damon (D): Mark, you look sad today, what's going on?

Mark (M): It's a problem at home, it's embarrassing. See, I've always been virile, no problems in the sack, you know? But recently, maybe it's stress at work or something, I just haven't been able to do it as much.

D: Do it?

M: Get hard, get erections, they don't happen as much as before. I notice it, Kerry notices it.

D: Does she complain about it?

M: No, she's very good about it, she's always very loving, saying "it's no big deal" and all that. It's my issue, though. My doctor says I'm healthy, I'm not sick or anything. I just get frustrated when I can't get it up.

D: How often are you getting erections?

M: I still get them several times a week. I'm still attracted to my wife, and I can still get excited with her. But there's been a lot of stress lately, as you know. My job, the baby, my mother has been sick, a lot's been going on. Then when I can't make love to my wife, that just makes everything so much worse. I get frustrated, I feel depressed, like I'm less of a man. My doctor offered me a pill, but I shouldn't need a pill to make love to my wife. I should always be able to get an erection any time, any place.

D: Okay, Mark, I'm hearing a lot of "shoulds" today. I'm hearing you talk about being frustrated, even depressed, about a very real problem you're dealing with. What I'm seeing is that you are making this problem a lot worse with the way you're seeing it right now. The shoulds you are assigning to the problem may in fact be sustaining it! Can we look at those shoulds together?

M: Yeah, we can do that.

D: Alright. So let's look at the idea, "I should always be able to get an erection any time, any place," okay?

M: Fine, it's just a little embarrassing talking about it here. I'm a man, I should be able to just have them without talking about it in therapy.

D: Well, let's look at that. To begin, Mark, how did you learn this should, that you should always be able to get erections any time, any place?

M: How did I learn it? What do you mean?

D: I mean it can be helpful when we look at how we've learned the ideas we carry. None of us was born into this world believing, "I should always be able to get an erection whenever I want to." Somewhere along the way as men we learn this idea, we are taught it. Can you try to remember who first instilled this belief in you about your erections?

M: Who first did? Well, my earliest memory about this I guess would be in high school, in gym class. The guys who were having sex, the ones who talked about it whether it was true or not, seemed to be more powerful, more cool. It seemed like they were better than me somehow, since I wasn't having sex then, and couldn't lie about it. The fact that they could get it up and get it in seemed to bring them status somehow. Then in college, I felt very important if I could sexually please a young woman. Like I may not be the best looking guy, or the most athletic, I may not be the best dresser or have the most money. But here was my one thing I could really do, I could get it hard and have control.

D: Control, that seems to be an underlying belief here, that you should be in control of your body. Is this true ?

M: Oh yeah, I'd say so.

D: Okay, so what I'm hearing so far is that this belief about being in control of your erections stems from peers in high school and college. Can you tell me what this culture says to you about this?

M: Well, society is always telling us that we should be in control. Control of our jobs, our wives, our money. And yes, it says we should always be in control of our bodies and our erections.

D: And what happens if one doesn't have this control?

M: Then, well...then he's nothing. He has no control, no one wants to be around him. No one wants to love him.

D: Ah, so again, I'm hearing a Core Belief being articulated. Underneath the idea that "I should be in control of my body including my erections" is a deep rooted fear. Can you articulate that fear?

M: That if I'm not in control, I won't be loved.

D: Excellent! I think you really hit the nail on the head there. So again, Mark, let's come back to this idea. How is this message that you should be in control being communicated to you now?

M: Everywhere you go, it's there. The advertisements you see on TV, in the magazines, constantly demonstrate this. That you should be muscular, in shape, in control, or else.

D: Or else?

M: Yeah, or else no one can love you.

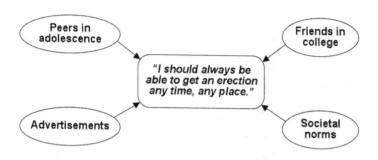

D: Okay, so now you're really starting to see how a combination of external factors have taught you this belief, and there's probably even more we haven't discussed yet. But let me ask you this, do you think this is true for all men everywhere? Should all men be able to get erections whenever they want to, 24/7? Should all men be in control of their bodies like that all the time?

M: Well, no.

D: Really, why not?

M: Well, I'm not sure (pauses). Okay, not all men need to have an erection all the time, because no work would get done if we did (laughs). But also, we're not machines either. We're human. I've known guys, sometimes older guys, who really don't see this as such an issue, they know who they are with or without hard-ons. They have good days and bad days, it doesn't mean they're less than or unlovable. See, it's easier for me to say that about others than it is myself.

D: Yes, but that's the point of that question. To take you out of the equation for a moment. To pull out what is objective versus subjective. It is objectively true that no man can get an erection whenever he wants to his entire life. What is problematic is the subjective opinion you derive from that, that somehow it makes you less of a person, less able to be loved. If some men can simply accept the "ups and downs" that come with aging and go with their bodies wherever they are taken, why can't you?

M: I guess I can. I can try to anyway.

D: So then, Mark, who is profiting from this idea that you should be able to have erections any time you want? Who stands to win from your depression about this?

M: I'm not sure. What do you mean?

D: I mean anytime we carry shoulds on ourselves to the point of suffering and despair, there is someone or something on the sidelines that is gaining in some form. Can you think who or what can gain from your thought that you should have an erection anytime you want to?

M: Well, certainly the drug companies you see everywhere. In the magazines, during the football commercials, they all want you to say to yourself, "Dude, you should get it up any where any time." So in that way, I think they're making quite a profit on it.

D: Yes! I would expand that to say the drug companies are banking on you being afraid of being unlovable in order to make a profit. They carefully spend billions of dollars on advertising each year with the intent of communicating one clear goal: Get erections or you won't be loved.

M: Yeah, they're everywhere.

D: So, then, when I ask you, how do you feel when you think, "I should be able to get erections any time, any where," how do you feel?

M: I feel lousy, I feel discouraged, because I just can't any-more. I don't know if I'll ever have that control again. There are times I can and times that I can't. When I say I "should," though, I feel really down.

D: Right. So now we have talked about how badly it feels to believe this, how you've learned to believe this, and who is profiting from it. Now I'd like to know what it would be like to go one day without this should? To wake up in the morning and not have this should hanging over you?

M: It would be really great, actually. It would be such a relief, I'd be a lot more relaxed. And, chances are, if I was a lot more relaxed then I'd be more likely to get hard!

D: See how that works? You are conditioned to think a certain way about erections which almost guarantees you're less likely to have them.

M: Yeah, and like you said, there are plenty of folks who want to make money off my fear. But if I didn't have this should, then I wouldn't have this fear.

D: I would certainly agree with that. So, Mark, now let me check with you, who would you be if you didn't have this should about yourself?

M: I'd be a lot more confident, I'd be a lot more relaxed. I think I'd be someone who can just relax with his wife without all that anxiety and fear lingering about. I could enjoy myself a whole lot more.

D: So, how do you feel now that we've talked about this?

M: Better, more hopeful, like I don't have to make such a big deal about something I've been told to make such a big deal about.

D: Good, good. Now, the last step here is to replace the wording of the statement, "I should be able get an erection any time, any place." Based on what we have talked about today, how can you rephrase so that it does not cause you anxiety or fear?

M: I could say, "I could have a erection."

D: Okay. Anything else you can say?

M: Well, another way to say it is, "I'd prefer to have control of my erections. But if I don't, I'm still lovable, and there are still other ways to please my partner."

D: Wonderful! How does it feel to make that statement?

M: Powerful. Like I'm not going to give the power to my erections to determine if I'm lovable or not. Whether I have one or not, I'm still a good person.

Mark began by investing in the messages he and most men receive at an early age: You should always be able to get an erection and you should always be in control. He came to understand the depression and despair this thought was causing him, and how this suffering in fact impacted his ability to have erections. This is representative of what many men and women do. By trying so desperately to control an outcome, they almost guarantee that the outcome will never take place.

CHAPTER 7
TIPS FOR BEING ABSOLUTELY SHOULD-LESS IN EVERYDAY LIFE

Now that you have read this far, what is the first thing you can do to have an easier day? What follows are some tips for inquiry, and dealing with obstacles to living absolutely should-less.

Everyday living will give you ample chance to challenge and dispute shoulds. Just turning on the television or leaving your home will immediately expose you to advertising which aims to make you as uncomfortable and miserable as possible so that you will spend money. You will be dealing with people in your life, perhaps family members, coworkers, or even good friends, who will say or do things to should you, perhaps without even realizing it.

It may not always be obvious when you are being bombarded with shoulds. A good tip is to be aware of your feelings as much as possible. Instead of trying to distract yourself with television or movies, or alter your brain chemistry with caffeine, alcohol, or any other substance, try just being present with an uncomfortable feeling. Whenever you feel nervous, sad, guilty, anxious, or angry, these are absolutely the best times to explore the should that is causing it. Journal writing routinely is a useful tool, and can be especially helpful when you are experiencing a strong painful feeling. You can get more clarity at these times as to how you are making yourself miserable.

Write down as many shoulds as you can. It doesn't have to be legible, rational, or even have to make sense to anyone but you. Just let your mind go free and get it out. It may be something personal like, "that guy at work shouldn't talk to me like that," or "that doctor on the news shouldn't be getting prosecuted for helping terminal patients die," or "people on the street should smile back at me when I smile." Then go back to chapter 3 and go through the steps.

Holidays, especially Christmas, are the perfect time to practice living life absolutely should-less. During the last six weeks of every year, regardless of your religion, all of us are bombarded with an excessive flurry of shoulds coming at us in all directions. Family, media, coworkers, department stores, pretty much everywhere you look the message is clear: "You should be buying things." The consequence of this is that it results in many people feeling guilty, sad, inadequate, even unlovable, like Rosa in the vignette earlier in the book.

For many, spending an excessive amount of money is simply not possible. I know parents who spend the entire year working, struggling, and sacrificing in order to provide food, clothes, safe housing, heat, and school supplies for their children. An admirable feat, definitely. But then Christmas comes around and guess what? None of that matters. Because adults and kids are all getting the same message—gifts are more important than love. "You should give your children expensive gifts to let them know how much you love them." See anything faulty about this logic?

There is an easier way to live in this life. You can challenge the status quo by choosing to be should-less, and even opting not to give presents if that would be a compromise to your happiness (or for you wallet!). Unfortunately, choosing to be happier with fewer shoulds can involve some rejection and disapproval from others. Deciding one year not to buy Christmas presents, or give birthday gifts, or not to send a card for any "holiday" invented by the card companies, can make you rather unpopular in your family. Any time someone breaks away from the status quo they risk some social consequences. As Senator John Edwards has said, "Any time you speak out powerfully for change, the sources of status quo attack."[2] If you are concerned about this, please keep the following in mind:

TIPS FOR RESISTING GIFT GIVING SHOULDS

1. This is your life and your life only. Relatives and friends may judge you for not spending money, but they won't pay your bills a month later.

2. People may be thrown off center when you think or act differently. They may react with surprise or hostility. But the ones in your life who truly care about you will see how much happier you are. They will want to support you in living a peace-filled life, and not going into great amounts of debt.

3. Sometimes it is better not to give others everything they want for holidays or birthdays. In fact, by always giving someone gifts at these times, you may unwittingly be sending them a message that love should be expressed primarily through material gifts.

---

[2] New Hampshire Democratic Debates televised by CNN on January 5, 2008

4. It can be quite beneficial to teach others, especially children, how to save and budget their own money. If they are always getting the gifts they want, then there is no reason for them to learn how to financially plan.

5. By not giving in to societal shoulds, you may be helping someone else in ways you can't even realize. By acting in a healthy way, you give others permission to do the same. There may be someone in your family suffering more financial duress than you, who finds incredible relief when you're the first one to stand up against holiday/birthday shoulds. Her shame about her financial situation may have prevented her from speaking up, but because you have done it, that road is paved.

Also remember to please be patient with yourself during this process. This is going against the grain of what most of us were conditioned to believe at an early age. Living absolutely should-less is a radically different way to live in the world. Most of us, myself included, don't have it in us to go against the grain every moment of every day.

There are times when I find myself on a should overload. Days when I am constantly looking around and shoulding the way my coworkers act, the way people on the subway smell, the way guys at the gym grunt. My partner is quite adept at asking me, "Do you feel like being right or being happy right now?" Well, honestly, sometimes the answer is, "Today I feel like being right!"

The difference between this and when I was younger is that now I know that when I suffer I am making a choice. I may choose to be "right" at times, but I also know that I'll suffer the consequences—stress, stomach pain, and/or insomnia. And I also am aware that I can pull myself out of this hell any time I choose.

If you find yourself regularly choosing to be right over being happy, I encourage you to demonstrate some compassion toward yourself. It is not the intention of this book to have you should yourself for having shoulds! If you find yourself struggling, please keep the following in mind:

TIPS FOR WHEN YOU ARE CHOOSING TO BE RIGHT OVER HAPPY:

1. Remember we were born and raised in a world that conditioned us to have shoulds long before we even had the words for it.

2. Everyday is a new beginning. If you shoulded constantly yesterday, you can start anew today.

3. If you are surrounded by others who should all day, it may be especially challenging to do otherwise. Remember, we are social animals. Moods are contagious. Notice what you do when someone across the room is yawning. In the same way, when someone around you is constantly choosing suffering over happiness, it takes extra effort not to do the same.

4. It can be very helpful to surround yourself with people who understand and support what you are trying to do. Making friends with people or gravitating more toward others who are trying to do the work, too, can help. You may know someone at work who always just seems happier than others. Try learning what their secret is.

5. There are certain physical / chemical states that can pose unique challenges to deciding to feel better. Hunger and fatigue are strong obstacles to choosing peace. If you are under the influence of a drug, or in the week after you've stopped using a mind-altering drug (including legal drugs such as caffeine or nico-

tine), then choosing happiness over righteousness can be quite difficult. Conversely, if you have a chemical imbalance and are not taking a prescribed psychiatric medication, then thinking rationally may be intensely challenging. Poor diet, chronic physical pain, or hormonal changes (at any age) can all be obstacles to choosing peace. Be patient, write in your journal, practice the steps to living Absolutely Should-less. Most importantly, forgive yourself.

In my own life and professional practice, I have come to understand that without fear, shoulds simply could not exist. One of the gifts our shoulds can give us is that they often illuminate and point out long held fears and beliefs. For instance, any time you are still shoulding yourself, try asking, "or else what?" What's really the worst that can happen?

During the course of writing this book, there have been times I have thought, "I should go to the gym tonight." I may say to myself, "or else what?" And the answer of course is always the same, "or you'll be out of shape, and no one will love you." Quite a leap, isn't it? Is it true that no one would ever love me the rest of my life if I miss one night at the gym? Of course not. But in this way, my should just gave me insight into a huge fear that I and many others share. It makes me want to thank the should for showing this to me. That is, before I squash it with the seven steps mentioned in chapter 3.

At the same time, we do live in a world in which we encounter many unexpected and painful tragedies. The media loves to report on stories in which people are hurt or killed by unexpected illnesses, violence, accidents, and natural disasters. Of course such events will provoke feelings of fear or uncertainty. How can we use our thoughts effectively in these cases?

1. Discipline and focus. If you practice the seven steps outlined in Chapter 3 and consistently do your journal writing, then the events and tragedies of the world will not have as strong an impact. You may feel pain and loss, but the feelings will not be so overwhelming without the should attached.

2. Talk about it with others. Some people in your life will try to get you back into shoulding anytime you start to experience some peace (remember the concept of "homeostasis" discussed in chapter 3). But others will find this process interesting, want to try being absolutely should-less themselves, and will want to support you on your quest to live a more joyful life. Surround yourself with these people—it is very hard for any of us to do this alone.

3. Continue to recognize the media's role in your fears. Be vigilant with the shoulds that are sold to you every day, and the fears behind the advertising campaigns. Note that for every actual tragedy the media covers, there are millions and millions of people who are living life safely today.

4. Try to recognize the fear behind the shoulds that you give to yourself. What is the "or else" behind the shoulds you tell yourself? Try to recognize your investment in the status quo when you should others.

5. Recognize that there is often a good reason why bad things happen. This is a very difficult concept to comprehend, especially when you are experiencing tremendous amounts of grief and sadness. But take a look at all the good things in your life today. How many of these did you plan? Have you ever had something go

horrifically wrong in your life, only years later to say, "it's a good thing that happened?"

Most fear is related to thoughts about something that has not even happened. As discussed in chapter 2, whenever you express any kind of opinion on a future event, you are practicing the power of faith. Writing this book has a been a constant reminder of this power. There are times when my thoughts have been, "Why are you doing this? No one cares about your ideas about shoulds, no one is going to read this or be helped by this." The consequence of choosing to think this is that I have felt discouraged and frustrated. But when I use the power of my thoughts to reply, "I think there are ideas here that can help some people. If only one person feels better it was worth it. I may never know the effects of putting out these ideas into the world," then I feel hopeful, charged up, encouraged. In either scenario, the way I feel is completely determined by how I decide to utilize the power of my faith.

If you use the power of your faith to decide that life is going to be wonderful, or at the minimum manageable, then shoulds become completely obsolete. Shoulds cannot thrive in a heart that is open to knowing everything is working out for the best—even when you are not getting something or someone you want. In the beginning of your practice you may only have small moments where you truly feel this knowledge. Again, be patient. Staying sane in an insane world is a full time job, but I promise you it is possible, and it will pay off.

CHAPTER 8
REAL PEOPLE VERSUS THEIR SHOULDS –
MIA FIGHTS THE SYSTEM

Mia is a 24-year-old lesbian graduate student of Polish descent, who comes for counseling for a non specified anxiety problem. She is getting her M.A. in political science, and is very active in campus politics. She recently was denied insurance on her partner's insurance plan because her company does not honor domestic partnerships.

Mia (M): It's insane, I'm telling you. Those greedy oppressors want to keep their heads in the sand. But it's wrong, simply wrong, they should not discriminate against same sex partners, they shouldn't practice archaic forms of hatred against us.

Damon (D): You seem pretty angry about this.

M: Of course I'm damned angry about this. This is my life we're talking about, this is no game.

D: Yes, I can see that. But Mia, let me ask you, do you enjoy being this angry all time?

M: Honestly? No. I do not enjoy being this angry all the time. Sometimes, yeah I do. But all the time? No. I wish I could just turn it on and turn it off at will, you know?

D: Yes I do. And if you allow me, I think I can help you do that. To utilize your anger and outrage when it helps you, but turn it off when it doesn't. Are you willing to try that with me?

M: Sure, if you think you can do it.

D: No, I think you can do it once we do it together. Now, you mentioned earlier a major should—"they shouldn't discriminate against same sex couples," and an outcome of that should was feeling some uncontrolled anger. Am I accurate so far?

M: Yes, I believe so.

D: Okay. Now Mia, without agreeing or disagreeing with the content of that statement, I'm just curious to know, how did you learn that? How did you learn that these corporations shouldn't be discriminating against same sex unions?

M: How did I learn it? I just know it. What do you mean how did I learn it? Do you think they should be discriminating against same sex couples? You think that's like, uh, mentally healthy for them to do that?

D: Now, remember, I'm not stating an opinion, I'm simply opening up the "should" for inquiry. Sometimes by learning more about our views we get a more solid understanding of where they come from, and it can even help us teach them to others.

M: Right, O.K., good. How did I learn it? Well, just being a lesbian in this world kind of makes you go in that direction. And my partner, of course; Toni feels very strongly about this. And my family. They've always been pretty liberal; that's why they wanted to come to this country. I was always raised to believe that everyone deserves equal treatment and equal benefits.

D: Great. Anyone else?

M: Well, my professors, of course, and the other students in class.

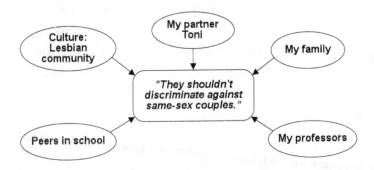

D: O.K., good. Now let me ask you—do you believe this is true for everyone everywhere 24/7? That the corporations shouldn't discriminate against anyone for same sex protection?

M: Indeed I do. I truly believe that is how it should be. That everyone should get equal health coverage and protection.

D: And when you say this, when you talk about this should, how does it feel?

M: Well, like I said before, I get pretty pissed off. Because even though it's true, it's not the way things are right now as I just so pleasantly found out.

D: True. So when you get angry, where do you feel it most in your body?

M: Where? Oh, my upper back, around the shoulder area? It kills at times like these. It's hurting today. And I get these headaches, migraines maybe? They're intense, I have to lie down. I notice I'm prone to get those a lot more often when I'm angry about something.

D: Interesting. Are there any other disadvantages of carrying anger?

M: Yeah, I don't eat as much. Though that can be a good thing, you know? But the reason I don't eat as much is because my stomach hurts sometimes, I don't sleep so well, I'm more likely to have a short fuse with Toni, I don't concentrate so well in class if I haven't slept well, I can't see a doctor about any of this because I can't get insurance, so you could say there are some disadvantages.

D: And what are the advantages?

M: Well, (pause), I often think that it gives me a kind of energy that I wouldn't have otherwise. Even if I am tired and burned out, it keeps me going. You know, I want to make a difference on this planet somehow.

D: Yes, I can see that. So, we started by talking about how your should about companies that discriminate against same sex couples leads to anger, and how anger leads to stomach aches, insomnia, problems in school, and problems in home. Yet, as you said, anger can also be a motivator at times. Is it possible to be motivated to help change the world without the intensity of the anger?

M: I think so, I think that's possible.

D: Now, I'm curious, Mia. As you well know as a political science student, history is filled with people profiting or benefiting from other people's misery right?

M: Oh yeah.

D: So, in this case, who is profiting when you suffer from your anger?

M: Certainly the companies that make the pain relievers and the Pepto, that's for sure. The guys who manufacture Ambien must be doing well off me by this point. The corporations that refused us the same sex benefits in the first place, they are definitely profiting because if I did have insurance I'd be going to go see a doctor and dealing with these problems. They're saving money by discriminating against me. And... you profit, too.

D: Me?

M: Yes, you. And this clinic. You are profiting because I'm so stressed out I have to come here every week.

D: Excellent point. It sure doesn't seem like you are benefiting much, though, or Toni.

M: No, it sure doesn't.

D: So bottom line, Mia: These shoulds you carry, these impossible rigid expectations you have are hurting you. They're not helping others. You don't serve the world by being a martyr. There are times when all of us need to ask ourselves—do I want to be right today or do I want to be happy? Everyone may agree that you're right, but they won't have your migraines for you. When reality conflicts with shoulds, as it always seems to do sooner or later, this is the time to start practicing acceptance for how things are.

M: But what do you want me to do, just stop caring about injustice in the world? Just lie back and say fine, I'm not going to stress myself out anymore while people like me and you get shit on everyday?

D: It's interesting you say that. You make it sound like the world will go to hell in a hand basket if you had less anger and more peace.

M: Well?

D: One of the biggest mistakes politically active individuals make is thinking they can change the world by attacking others and self-destructing. Many people think that letting go of shoulds and practicing acceptance is the same as giving up and doing nothing, when in fact the exact opposite is true.

M: Run that by me again?

D: Let me ask you this—how do you feel when someone's telling you what you should think or should believe about what is happening in Iraq or any current event?

M: I tell them, "Screw you up a phone pole, I'll think what I want."

D: Right! So then how do you think the heads of these corporations respond to you when you do the same thing ?

M: Ah, I think I see where you're going with this.

D: Almost no one opens their minds or hearts when they feel they are being challenged or attacked. When we look back historically on many political movements, we tend to focus on a few violent angry protests that had an impact. And it makes sense. This country was founded on violent, angry, bloody protests. But what history generally does not teach is how quiet, gentle, respectful, calm talks and loving actions have helped to change legislature's minds, and helped shape public opinions in a different direction. Rosa Parks, Gandhi, even Martin Luther King, Jr. taught this. We tend to think that in order to make a difference, we must rage, attack, and should those who stand in our way. Most of the time though, when you attack someone, their opposition to you just gets stronger.

M: Like, you get more bees with honey than vinegar. So maybe, by going on the attack with others, I'm actually accomplishing less?

D: And by allowing your anger to devour you, I'd definitely say you're accomplishing less. Hunger and fatigue make it nearly impossible to think rationally; that's why it's used so effectively with political prisoners. When you do it to your-self, is that really helping the world around you?

M: It doesn't seem that way.

D: So let me ask you for a moment to imagine one day, only one day, in which you wake up, and the shoulds about how others are discriminating and abusing power don't exist. Just one day, mind you. What would it feel like to wake up that day?

M: It's hard to imagine that. But I think it would be great. Like a huge burden off my aching shoulders.

D: Good. Stay with that with for a few minutes here. Let me also ask you to consider who you would be if you didn't have this should?

M: Who would I be? (pause). I don't know. I really don't know. I'm sorry, I don't have an answer for you.

D: That's O.K., that's quite alright. It's interesting though, isn't it? Without that should, your sense of identity is unclear. Without the anger, you don't know who you are.

M: True. But as you said, it's that anger that's actually get-ting in the way of school, of my relationship, of my health, of actually having an impact on others. You know, as you were talking earlier, I was remembering how I got involved in politics in the first place. My first women's studies profes-sor in undergrad was one of the most kindest, gentlest, and most intelligent people I've ever known. She got me really interested in seeing the world as it is, with all the unfairness and injustice. But she didn't speak out from an angry place. She talked in a very giving, almost loving way. Even with-out anger, she still had a tremendous impact on me, maybe more of an impact. She didn't tell us what to think, she just told us what was going on and let us decide what to do with that information.

D: Ah, so she taught without shoulds, right?

M: Yeah, she never had a should about it. Yet she was one of the most effective teachers there, and in her own way is changing the world. She certainly changed mine. So, maybe there is a way to help the world without shoulding and attacking others.

D: Yes, I would agree with this. Now, keeping that in mind, let's go back to the original should that was upsetting you so much earlier. "They shouldn't discriminate against same sex couples." On a scale of 1 to 10, how angry were you when we started?

M: Oh, I'd say I was at a 9.5.

D: O.K., and how about now?

M: Now, it's more like a 5. It's there, but it's more manageable.

D: Excellent! And this is the key to what you said you wanted earlier to manage your anger, to use it to your advantage. How did you get it from a 9.5 to a 5?

M: Well, like you said, realizing I don't have to be right, I don't have to be so angry, and if I am that angry, I'm really just getting in my own way.

D: Good, now the replacement. Can you think of another way to say, "they shouldn't discriminate against same sex couples" so that it's less rigid, more of a preference?

M: "I prefer that they stop discriminating against same sex couples. I hope they stop discriminating against same sex couples. I could be healthier if they would stop discriminating against same sex couples. I could see a stupid doctor already if they would stop discriminating against same sex couples." (laughs).

D: Good! How does that feel?

M: It feels better. I feel lighter. Like I'm more likely to sleep better tonight, make more of a difference tomorrow. I may not have the rights I want right now, but I'm going to feel better about it.

Mia's should illustrates a common conundrum. What if it's a should about others, and everyone around you agrees with it? Remember, as mentioned earlier in the book, I am not here to say that people should not should! What I do explore, however, are the consequences of such thinking, and how one's shoulds can be hurtful and cause needless pain.

Many people involved in political activism believe that the only way to bring about social change is to constantly should themselves and others. In Mia's case, it is clear that her shoulds were leading to more suffering, and ultimately sabotaging her goals to perform well in school, have a happy relationship, and help the world around her. She realized that at some point she was going to have to choose: did she want to be right—or did she want to be happy?

Are choosing happiness and activism mutually exclusive? Absolutely not. There are many ways you can affect the world from a place of peace and tranquility. You can do volunteer work. You can write a letter to you local lawmakers. You can go to peace rallies. You can contribute money to organizations that represent your issues. Or hey, you can even write a book! But if you infuse these activities with aggressive shoulds instead of peace, then it is less likely your voice will be heard.

CONSIDER THIS:

Stopping to ask yourself "Do I want to be right or happy" in any situation can lead you instantaneously to peace.

CHAPTER 9
A DAY IN THE ABSOLUTELY SHOULD-LESS LIFE

I know that it can be difficult to approach every problem in life from an absolutely should-less perspective. We get distracted, we get overwhelmed, we forget; we are constantly bombarded with information and pressured to accomplish more and more. But I also know firsthand that practicing life absolutely should-less can help to stay focused and clear-headed. It can also help you make healthy decisions in any given situation.

There are many times during the day when we are confronted with difficult or annoying situations. We don't always have time to slow down or stop go through the seven questions described in chapter 3. What we can do, however, is practice one or two of the steps in our heads, just enough to slow down our thoughts and reactions.

You have already read several vignettes from some of my counseling sessions. Now I am going to let you in on how I deal with conflicts "on the go" in my daily life. Just like you, I am nowhere near perfect in this process. But I can promise you I am

123

trying. And as these examples will show, continued mindfulness around questioning shoulds can make life's stressors and disappointments a lot easier. They do not make the problems go away, they just give us better tools to handle them.

I wake up at 7 a.m., feeling tired, cranky, and seriously not wanting to get out of my warm bed. Within 45 seconds of being awake, my shoulds are already on overload. "You shouldn't have to get out of bed today, you shouldn't be so tired, you should have more energy, you shouldn't have stayed up so late last night, you should take better care of yourself, you should get more sleep at night."

With shoulds this heavy, of course I'm feeling tired! I make it to my Cinnamon Toast Crunch and in my mind review some of the questions which help me focus.

How do you know you shouldn't have to go to work today? I don't, I really don't know how anything should be in the world. All I do know is that my thinking that things should be different from how they are leads me to feel even more tired and cranky. I am aware that the thought "I should have more energy" leads me to feel irritable, and it profits the societal norms. Realizing that it is only my shoulds causing me to be unhappy, and not the morning time, is enough to get me out of bed.

My partner turns on "The Today Show." I am told that global warming is a dangerous reality and that the ice caps are melting quickly. Flooding and disasters are inevitable; humans are devouring the environment and the outcome of this is guaranteed to be much suffering. "Global warming shouldn't be happening," I say to myself, and then I notice how this thought leads me to feel just as irritable and cranky as when I first woke up.

How do you know what you think you know about global warming? Well, Matt Lauer just told me about it so it must be true.

Once I realize the absurdity of my own thought, I notice that most of the commercials on this show are for pills that treat headaches, acid reflux, and colds. Suddenly I remember the question, *Who is profiting from your should?* I am reminded that although television can be a source of information and entertainment, it must also find a way to make money for the businesses that pay millions of dollars for a 15-second advertising spot. Scaring people about the destruction of the planet seems like an easy and effective way to get people to spend money on things they may not really need. This helps me remember to think critically about the investment the media has in my suffering and in buying medications to feel better. I then remember that I can use the power of my faith to decide that the world is coming to an end and feel miserable, or, I can use the power of my faith to decide that things are going to ultimately work out okay in the end. I decide on the latter.

So I get out of the house and down to the subway platform. I wait for the "E" uptown train, which seems to be taking longer to arrive today. By the time it comes the car is packed. I can barely nudge my way in, and then I am intimately pressed up against total strangers. I think, "They should add more trains in the morning. These people should just get out of my way." I realize I have a choice at this moment—*do I want to be right or happy?* If I want to be right then I know this will result in feeling even angrier. Because I choose happiness instead of righteousness this time, I ask myself some questions:

How does it feel to believe in this should? Angry, bitter, and resentful.

Who would you be without this should? I would be a patient person, with much more access to peace, who could simply ride the train without making a drama out of it.

Is there a part of you that wants to be that peaceful person? Indeed there is.

Is there a part of you that doesn't want to be that person? There could be. I have a history of being self destructive by holding on to the adrenaline ride of anger and grudges. There was once much secondary gain for me to do this since it meant I never had to take responsibility for my moods, and I always had a dramatic story to tell at work. Telling this story gave me energy and attention. Indeed there is an old part of me that enjoys being dramatic and bitter, but not as much anymore,

Replace it. I wish there were more trains. I'd prefer to have more room to stand. I'd kind of like to go to work one day without my feet getting stepped on. But despite these inconveniences I am glad I am not stressed in traffic, that I'm doing my part for the environment by not driving a car, and that I'm not spending a portion of my paycheck on gas.

As I think of these replacements, I feel a lot more relaxed. It doesn't change the fact that I'm on a crowded train. It doesn't change that fact that I get annoyed when I'm sandwiched against a stranger who is coughing in my face. But it does change my feelings about the situation. I may still feel annoyed, but not vehemently angry. I may still feel like this situation is beyond my control, but not victimized.

I manage to get to work on time. I've been at this job now for about six months, and really seem to be doing well. Or so I thought. My supervisor calls me into her office, with a question:

"You have been doing absent notes, right?"

"Absent notes?"

"Haven't you been doing absent notes when your clients don't come to your group?"

"Uh, no."

"Well, you should be doing them, you should always have absent notes in there, you should have known this."

Anger courses through my veins. Blood rushes to my head. I consider quitting. This is a really good sign for me that I need to walk away, breathe, and go through my should questions.

"She shouldn't be shoulding me about not doing something that I didn't know about," I think. "Why is she shoulding me about doing an absurd activity that makes no clinical sense whatsoever? She should get off my back, she should mess with someone else. I should walk out." After taking several deep breaths I'm able to go to my office and ask myself some questions quickly.

Do you want to be right or happy right now? I want to be happy.

How do you know she shouldn't be shoulding you? I don't know that she shouldn't be shoulding me. I do know that I am a complete hypocrite if I walk around saying "other people shouldn't should me." Just because I am in the process of challenging the shoulds in my life, and accessing more peace and happiness from this, it doesn't mean other people around me will want to do the same. Others have a right to practice their own critical shoulds; this is still a free country. Maybe she doesn't know any better. How would she, since this book hasn't been published yet? Just reminding myself that I don't have to burden myself with other people's shoulding is enough to calm me down

Replace it. I'd prefer that she stop shoulding me. I prefer that I stop shoulding me. I prefer that I stop shoulding her.

By going through this process I start to identify the real source of my frustration. It is not my supervisor's shoulds that is causing me to get upset, it is my shoulds that are the source of my anger. If I can challenge and change my own shoulds, then perhaps my supervisor and others can as well. Either way, I still have the choice and responsibility to alter my own thoughts, not anyone else's.

As I make my way home, I think, "You really should go to to the gym tonight." But I don't want to go to the gym. And telling myself I should go to the gym only leads me to feel more anxious and impatient. As I come back on the same crowded train returning home, I ask myself some questions.

How did you learn your should about the gym? I think about the images I see constantly in the media, that I should look thin, young, and toned if I want to be happy, loved, or successful.

And who is profiting from your should? The owners of the gym, of course. But so are the magazines and movies which instilled this should in me in the first place. Every time I go to the gym because I think I should, I am literally and figuratively buying into these media images that tell me I am not good enough as who I am. I am reinforcing the ideas that I should change myself to please others and perpetuate the status quo.

Do you really want to buy into that? No, this is where I have a choice. The same way I can question the motives of the sensationalizing media around global warming, I can also challenge any message I receive that tells me I should feel bad about myself if I don't conform to what others are doing.

Replace it. I prefer to go to the gym. It could be beneficial for me to go to the gym. I may feel better if I go to the gym tonight. But whether I go or not, I am still a valuable loving person. I will not allow other people or institutions to decide how I feel about myself.

So with that insight I decide not to go to the gym.

Instead I call my friend Ruth in California. She was diagnosed eight months earlier with pancreatic cancer, and at this point is no longer taking chemotherapy treatments. She and I both know she is going to die. I hang up the phone and cry. I say to myself, "It's not fair, Ruth shouldn't be dying." I decide to do some questioning.

How do you know this is true? Because this is an amazing woman who has given most of her 63 years to helping others. She has so much vitality and love in her, this shouldn't be happening.

How do you feel when you think this should? I feel worse than before. I feel helpless, angry, discouraged.

Do you want to keep feeling this way? Is this honoring Ruth and what she has stood for? No.

How did you learn this should? While asking this question I realize that I don't know why most things happen on this earth, especially not death. I just know I am affected by social norms which tell me one should live as long as possible. That does not mean it is universally true.

Who would you be without this should? I would be someone who is more accepting of what is happening and less at war with reality.

Replace it. I wish Ruth would stay alive. It hurts me that she is going to die. But I know that sometimes things happen for reasons I do not understand. I can instead choose to honor Ruth by being absolutely should-less with my grief and helping others learn tools for reducing their own sorrow.

When I change my mind like this, I am motivated to continue to work on this book. When I sit and think about how things shouldn't be happening, I just want to escape. This doesn't mean I don't feel hurt or pain. It does mean I can feel the loss and sadness without the added layer of despair or anger that comes from telling myself "this shouldn't be happening." This is the freedom that comes from practicing absolutely should-less thinking in all the conflicts in my daily life.

Is this hard to do? Yes. Does it take will and discipline? Yes. But is it worth it? Definitely yes. Any one of these examples would have previously sent my mind spiraling about the cruel and unfair world we share. I could have spent days ruminating about them and losing large amounts of sleep before I finally let them go. Asking myself these questions and going through at least a few of the steps saves time and energy. I can rest easier, I can focus better, I can face hardships and take clearer action to handle them.

CHAPTER 10
TAKING THE NEXT STEP

L ife doesn't have to be that hard. Now you know why. Now you understand how to use the power of your own thoughts to have a better day.

As you have read through this book, you may have thought how these ideas could help others you know. Perhaps you have friends or relatives who seem stuck in their misery, maybe co-workers who suffer from being too rigid or critical of themselves and others.

I have learned that the very best way to truly integrate new information into my brain is to share it with others. Staying absolutely should-less in this world is such a different way to think, and is nearly impossible to do alone. By talking about these concepts with others and supporting each other in taking these steps, you are helping yourself and the people around you ascend. Remember, moods are contagious; no one is an island. When you share these ideas with others, you are then helping the individuals and the environment around you, and that will make your own tasks much easier.

There are many creative ways people have told me they have shared these ideas with others:

— One young woman was having a considerably difficult time getting along with her mother with whom she lived. They

131

would fight over who would do the laundry, wash the dishes, and have control over the remote. She came to me one day and told me that she and her mother agreed to have one "no should" day around the house. Based on the question, "What would one day be like without this should?" they agreed to find out. She happily described to me a day in which they did not fight, and actually enjoyed each other's company. They liked it so much they agreed to try two days completely should-less.

— One man told me about the "Should Pies" he made with his spouse every time they found themselves shoulding each other. Based on the question, "How do I know this should is true?" they learned they could empathize with each other's position better when they both took responsibility for the familial and cultural factors that led to the shoulds they brought into the relationship.

— I've led groups in which people made collages about the benefits their shoulds have for others. Based on the question, "Who is profiting or benefiting from my should?" I have had people cut out ads from magazines and newspapers symbolizing who is profiting off their shoulds about themselves and their appearance. This serves as a visual reminder of who is gaining every time you negatively pass judgment on yourself and others.

— Some people in relationships take turns challenging each other with the all the questions outlined in chapter 3. Especially in couples where tension and resentment has built up, it can be quite relieving when two people can ask each other these questions and listen respectfully to the answers.

— I mentioned my own "no-shoulds" sign I once wore for a week in chapter 1. If this is not possible for you, try carrying a "no-shoulds" sign in your wallet, your dashboard, bathroom mirror, or any location where you are bound to see it several times throughout the day. The idea is to make the exercise creative, fun, and helpful for you and your loved ones. If you find a new way to do this, please let me know at www.shouldless.com.

I have mentioned that we live in a society in which we are conditioned early on in life to judge ourselves and others quite negatively. I have talked about how the media, the society, even sometimes family members profit from such critical shoulds. How do these systems ever change?

The only way systems change is if individuals inside the systems change. You may ask, "how can one person like me make a difference in changing anything?" Indeed the only way change has ever happened is by individuals like you challenging their thoughts, changing their minds, and then sharing these new ideas with others. You are then being proactive in challenging the status quo and helping others see there can be an easier way to live in this world.

Consider now, the three people in your life you think could benefit the most from living life absolutely should-less:

1. _____

2. _____

3. _____

When the time is right, contact them. Give them a copy of this book, try one of the exercises listed above, or simply share with them what you have learned. By discussing your ideas and helping others, you are making this an easier and more tolerant world to live in.

Life isn't going to be that hard for any of us anymore. Let's start using the tools we have now to have a better day. After reading this, you could put this book away on the shelf and let it get dusty. Or, you also could periodically reread it, constantly perform the seven steps, and talk about it with others. Whatever your choice is, I truly hope that practicing life absolutely should-less fills your life with more joy, fun, and love.

AK
ACKNOWLEDGMENTS

- -

First and foremost I must thank my parents Joy and Paul Jacobs, two of the kindest, smartest, and generous individuals I will ever know. Thank you for all your guidance and patience while raising a stubborn kid like me.

I would like to thank my friends who read early drafts this book and offered me support and editorial advice: David Manis, Sara Reis, Jim Gaylord, Sheryl Sandler-Lopin, and Laura Harrison. I would especially like to thank Wendy Brown and Ryan Lennon, who in addition to reading this book, have listened patiently to all my wild theories about shoulds over the past decade, and given me unwavering encouragement and support.

The ideas in this book were inspired by the brave words and ideas of many who came before me. For this I must express gratitude to Bettina Aptheker, Dr. Aaron Beck, Dr. David Burns, Cher, Margaret Cho, Dr. Albert Ellis, Jacob Glass, Dr. Lee Jampolsky, Byron Katie, Dolly Parton, and Marianne Williamson.

I have been fortunate enough to have received personal and spiritual guidance by some outstanding professionals who helped me to challenge the "status quo" and learn to believe in myself. For this reason, I am so thankful to Margaret Benson Thompson, Ginny and Tim Fitzmaurice, Charles "Andy" Hauck, Alesia Kunz, Joe McHugh, Joni Migdal, A. Patrice Monsour, and Shari ReVille. Without your contributions I would not be the therapist or human I am today.

This book could not have been written if I had not received certain professional opportunities. There are not enough ways to express how thankful I am to Dr. David Lundquist and his decision to nurture my passion for group therapy. I also give infinite thanks for the assistance of Elena Moser, Dr. Kami Bryant, Chris Deluca, Rachel Stein, and Annie Mendelsohn. The book that sits before you would not exist without their support.

I have been blessed with many friends who also have contributed to the elimination of shoulds from my life. Thank you to Seema Suturwala, Jay Schwartz, Lisa Maslowe, Erica Gaudet Hughes, Ellen Hausner, my Patio Cafe "Sisters", Patrick McRae, Mary Robinson, Melissa Egan, Jules Tuyes, Chris Bender, Mark Charbonneau, Albert Gonzalez, Henry Kriegel, Michael Lehrman, and Jen Marchand. Very special thanks to all the members of the Jacobs, Arrow, and Ducat families for your patience and support—even when I haven't been around.

I am especially thankful to my editor Edward Hayman for his feedback and wisdom, as well as his fabulous wife Connie, for introducing us, and responding to my call for help. Much thanks to Ira Blutreich for helping to design the perfect Should-less cover.

A profound amount of gratitude goes out to David Hancock and the wonderful staff at Morgan James Publishing. Thank you for making this dream come true.

This book was written in loving memory of Jhan Dean Egg, Ruth Van Horn, Bill Thompson, and Ntombi Howell. I miss you all greatly, and hope these pages are a testament to your influence in my life.

Special acknowledgment must be given to Michael Santos, Sean Bumgarner, and Dr. Barbara McFarlane—thank you all for saving my life.

Thank you to Nancy Goldberg, aka "Goldie," for being the first adult to teach me how to challenge what I thought I knew to be "true." Your wise words to me in high school were the genesis of the ideas discussed in this book, and the key to my peace of mind in adulthood.

Thank you to Jason Jacobs, for being the best brother anyone could ever hope for.

Finally, I can't conceive of enough ways to express my loving gratitude and appreciation for Matt Cameron. Thank you for being my best friend, my partner, and my daily reminder that miracles are possible.

A free ebook edition is available with the purchase of this book.

To claim your free ebook edition:

1. Visit MorganJamesBOGO.com
2. Sign your name CLEARLY in the space
3. Complete the form and submit a photo of the entire copyright page
4. You or your friend can download the ebook to your preferred device

A **FREE** ebook edition is available for you or a friend with the purchase of this print book.

CLEARLY SIGN YOUR NAME ABOVE

Instructions to claim your free ebook edition:
1. Visit MorganJamesBOGO.com
2. Sign your name CLEARLY in the space above
3. Complete the form and submit a photo of this entire page
4. You or your friend can download the ebook to your preferred device

Print & Digital Together Forever.

Snap a photo

Free ebook

Read anywhere